To our valued customers,

We are proud to have been a part of Washington's growth for more than half a century. Much has changed in our industry since Associated Grocers started in 1934.

But not everything has changed. After 55 years, we are still committed to these ideals:

- Recognize that our success is dependent directly upon the success of our customers.
- Ensure our stockholders an excellent return on their investment.
- Provide our customers with a complete line of innovative and creative product programs at competitive prices.
- Offer a complete menu of professional retail support services.
- Cultivate a work environment that emphasizes respect for the individual, encourages teamwork and inspires employees to excel.
- Adhere to the highest ethical standards in all our business relationships.
- Recognize our corporate responsibility to contribute to the betterment of the community.

We believe that through our commitment to these standards we will continue to attract high caliber people and earn the business of our customers, thus assuring the long-term success of Associated Grocers.

Sincerely,

Don Benson
President

A Century of
Seattle's Business

In 1899, Robert Moran and his brothers built 12 stern-wheeled flatboats to carry miners up the Yukon River to the gold fields. Moran took them north as a fleet, losing one on the way.

A Century of Seattle's Business

James R. Warren

And the Staff of *Seattle Business* Magazine

Vernon Publications Inc.

Bellevue, Washington

ISBN 1-878425-00-5

Library of Congress Cataloging-in-Publication Data available

A Century of Seattle's Business is published by the Vernon Publications Book Division. Vernon Publications Inc. produces a wide range of business, regional and special-interest publications, including books and corporate histories; *Seattle Business* magazine, the official publication of the Greater Seattle Chamber of Commerce; *The Nurse Practitioner* journal; *Pacific Builder & Engineer* magazine; and several annual directories. For more information or to order individual or bulk copies of *A Century of Seattle's Business*, please contact:

3000 Northup Way, Suite 200
Bellevue, WA 98004
(206) 827-9900

Some of the material in this book appeared in slightly different form in *Seattle Business* magazine.

Author James Warren, Ph.D., is one of the area's foremost historians and director emeritus of Seattle's Museum of History and Industry. Additional material from *Seattle Business* magazine was written by Michele Dill, editorial director at Vernon Publications.

Special thanks to all the organizations and individuals who provided photographs for the book. They include: the Museum of History and Industry; John L. Scott, Inc.; Aldus Corp.; NeoRx Corp.; Port of Seattle; Airborne Express; Ben Thompson; *Seattle Post-Intelligencer*; University of Washington; *The Seattle Times*; The Boeing Company; PSF Industries; Koll Center Bellevue; Seattle City Light; Microsoft Corp.; PACCAR Inc.; Milliman and Robertson; Washington Natural Gas; Seattle-King County Convention & Visitors Bureau; and Puget Power.

Design and layout: Sandra J. Harner
Production coordination and design assistance: Candice Duncan Cross
Production management: Jon Flies
Writing/research assistance: Roberta Lang

Contents

In 1929, Third Avenue was decorated with scores of overhead signs
designating the retail outlets of small merchants, a rare sight in today's
downtown area.

Introduction

The development of business and industry in this region, while similar to that in other parts of the United States, has many unique aspects. Natural resources have been more abundant here than in many parts of America, and some of these resources, such as forests and the fisheries, are renewable if properly harvested. Washington is blessed with a great variety of soils and climates, resulting in one of the greatest varieties of farm crops of any of the states. Abundant hydroelectric power has attracted manufacturing enterprises. We have the Pacific Ocean as our doorstep. Our scenery is magnificent and unique. The list of regional advantages could continue for pages.

Yet during the last two decades of the 19th century, Puget Sound residents were concerned about problems all Americans were discussing. Among these concerns was the development of huge eastern business combines that controlled transportation and certain commodities. These virtual monopolies affected the lives of all who lived in the West by interfering with healthy competition in the marketplace. Consumers were very much aware of their lack of influence on the business world. Congressional leaders and other politicians heard their constituents and passed new laws to address those concerns.

The first King County Courthouse, built in 1882, was sold to the city in 1891 for use as a city hall. Haphazard additions resulted in it being called "the Katzenjammer castle."

But not before Washingtonians turned to the Populists and to the People's Party to fight this encroachment on their free way of living. Washington actually elected a third-party governor at the turn of the century and in the 1912 election a majority of Washington voters marked their ballots for Theodore Roosevelt, the third-party presidential candidate on the Progressive "Bull Moose" ticket.

The State of Washington was settled, for the most part, by an enlightened and energetic people—patriotic and honest folk who attempted to and usually succeeded in electing officials who promoted progressive ideals.

For example, the state was in the forefront of the effort to promote women's suffrage. In 1854, the year after Washington Territory was established, the territorial legislature debated the issue of women's suffrage and the vote for passage failed by only one vote. In 1883, Washington women were given the vote but lost it seven

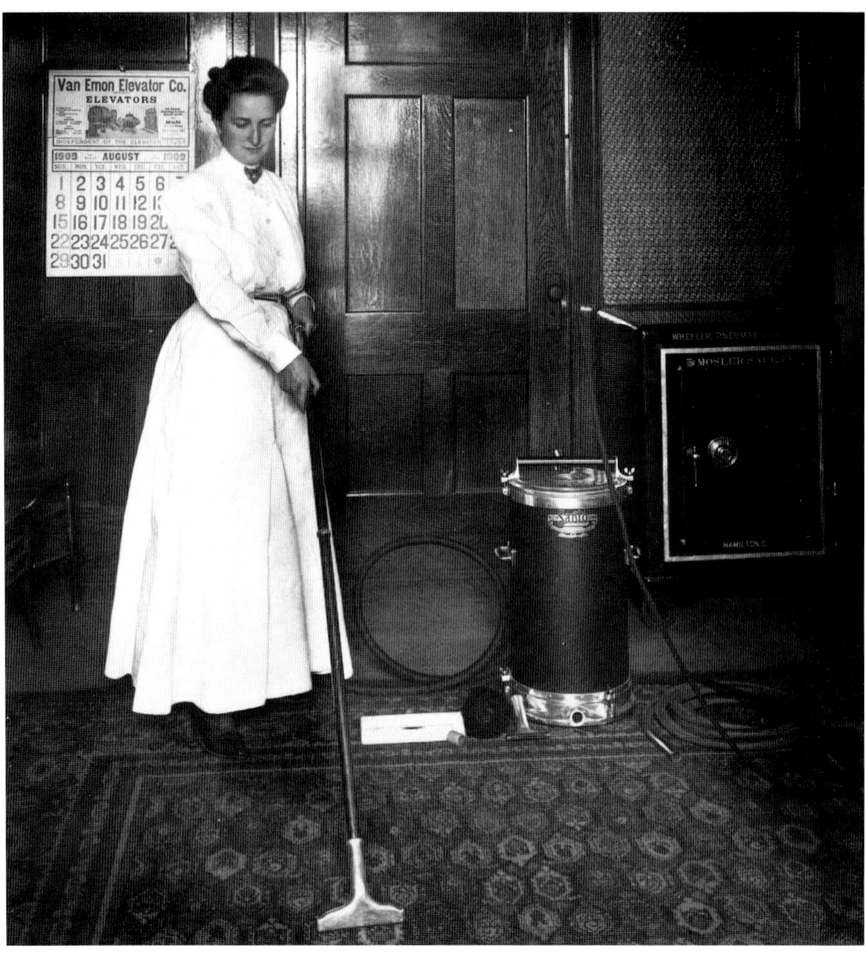

By 1909 the electric-powered vacuum cleaner was easing the chore of cleaning rugs.

years later in a state supreme court decision. In 1910, they again were allowed their suffrage—10 years before the U.S. Constitution was amended to allow all women citizens to cast ballots.

Before the turn of the century, Washingtonians agreed to equal educational rights. The "Barefoot Schoolboy Law" was passed, which in effect equalized tax collections on a statewide basis, allowing poorer districts the same funding per pupil as the wealthier districts.

The state developed many high schools before the turn of the century and at the same time funded the erection of colleges in all parts of the state. Citizens in pioneer days worried about the indigent and the mentally ill and voted for funding to build proper

As did every downtown street, Third Avenue near Marion received the attention of the regraders at the turn of the century. The building to the left of the Stander Hotel is the M.V.B. Stacy mansion, a boarding house at the time. The Chamber of Commerce had been housed there for a few years. Later, it was the site of the famous Maison Blanc restaurant.

Many a lumber schooner was loaded at Port Blakely Mill in the 1890s. One of these ships can be identified—the Colusa *out of San Francisco.*

Farmers' cooperatives were created to improve income for producers. They took root in the populist days before the turn of the century. Here is the Seattle building of the Washington Egg and Poultry Cooperative Association in the 1920s.

structures and provide for their care. In recent years, Washingtonians have developed a strong movement toward preservation of the environment and have shown a strong tendency to support individual rights, such as those of a woman to decide whether or not to bear a child.

On the other hand, Washingtonians have also revealed conservative streaks. They voted for prohibition in the state four years before the Volstead Act dried out the nation. And Washington remains one of only a few states refusing to legislate a graduated income tax. Polls indicate that more than half of Seattle's citizens are against busing children to schools outside their neighborhood.

Because of this mixture of the liberal and the conservative, Washington voters are strongly independent voters; they refuse to be labeled. They vote for what they believe is right.

The belief in the free enterprise system is endemic in the West. Vast numbers of citizens are involved with commerce, many in ownership positions, many more as employees who realize the important role of the free enterprise system in their way of life. Free enterprise may produce a sometimes bumpy road, but no other system comes even close to doing as well. Free enterprise is the only economic system that seems to work well with a democratic form of government.

We in the West tend to be an

independent lot anyway—not brash, just independent. We go our own way frequently. This is as true of business people as others. We figure things out for ourselves. If necessary, we sometimes move against the grain to reach our objectives. If a larger profit for the short term results in fewer customers eventually, our business leaders have a ready answer. After all, the customer is the most important ingredient in a business transaction. Therefore, most western businesses thrive on friendly service.

For the short history we possess, we have many "old" businesses. Seattle, with a history of but 137 short years, is home to many companies and corporations that trace their lineage back 100 years or more.

In the history of business on Puget Sound there have been some noted scalawags, but most went broke fast and some were run out of town in short order or stood before a judge and jury. Seattle's business community has policed itself well over the years.

Bekins Moving and Storage was still building its University District warehouse in this 1920s photo.

Let us spend the next few pages together discussing the businesses and services that developed in Seattle and the Puget Sound country from the founding years to the present day. And let us consider our good fortune at being able to develop this far Northwest corner of America beneath the umbrella of free enterprise.

The sweeping roof line of the Pike Place farmers' market in the mid-1920s leads the eye to the silhouette of the old armory beyond.

Part I

The Flow of History

In 1873, Commercial Street (now First Avenue South) was the heart of the business district. Atop the hill is the University of Washington, which opened its doors in 1861 on Arthur Denny's knoll. Among the increasing number of commercial establishments was the San Francisco Store on the right. This later became McDougall and Southwick department store, a Seattle landmark until after World War II.

Left inset: *Henry Yesler, Seattle's first industrialist, arrived in October 1852, seeking a waterfront location for his steam sawmill. Soon he was skidding logs down his shovel-shaped property on First Hill.*

Right inset: *Chief Seattle was in his mid-60s when Seattle's founders arrived. Realizing that the white man's diseases had decimated his people and believing that the Indians could not win any conflict with the white intruders, he preached to his people to keep the peace. He also cautioned the settlers to treat the land gently, for every part of it was sacred to his people.*

The Territorial Years— 1853-1889

The convergence of James Street and Yesler Way has been the site of many historic events. In 1875, the Occidental Hotel on the left divided the streets. The white structure at the end of the street on the west side of First Avenue is the Gem Saloon. Seattle's first newspaper, the Gazette, *was published here.*

Settlement of a new territory is a gradual process. First, a few pioneer families arrive and live what is primarily a self-sufficient existence. To earn income, they take advantage of the most obvious and accessible resources.

Settlers at Tumwater, Port Townsend, Seattle and other early settlements began felling the timber at water's edge and floating it as piling to ships or as logs for the first rudimentary sawmills. Within two decades, these pioneers were also mining coal in the foothills of the Cascades east of Puget Sound. In 1866, Columbia River salmon were preserved in tin cans for the first time. With this method of preservation, a vast improvement over salting and smoking, salmon soon developed as a major export.

As the population increased, it had to be fed, so agriculture became increasingly important. By happenstance, hops were found to thrive in the mild moist climate of Western Washington and soon carpeted the valley floors of the Puget Sound area. Once dried, hops could be transported long distances without spoilage, so they became the first major exportable crop from this area and were shipped not only to the eastern states but to England. The hop louse appeared, however, and ruined the fields west of the Cascades. But the higher elevations and drier climate east of the mountains kept the aphids away. To this day, Washington supplies about 80 percent of the hops used in the United States.

The Birth of Washington Territory

What is now the State of Washington was long known as Northern Oregon. It lay dormant until the question arose of whether the Oregon Territory was to belong to the United States or Great Britain. The War of 1812 ended with the Treaty of Ghent, which was signed in 1818. That agreement called for joint occupation of the Oregon country, which extended from the Rocky Mountains to the Pacific and from the southern tip of Russian Alaska at 54 degrees, 40 minutes, to the California border. This joint occupation continued until 1846.

Not until 1843 did many Americans find their way to this distant land beyond the Great American Desert (as the Great Plains were called) and the mighty Shining Mountains (as the Rockies were sometimes called). That year, more than 900 Americans crossed the plains and climbed over the mountains to reach the Willamette Valley. This was the first large American migration. For the first time, American settlers began to outnumber the personnel of the Hudson's Bay Company in Oregon.

In 1846, as the Ghent Treaty required, President James K. Polk provided the British with one year's notice that America intended to end the joint occupation. Furthermore, Polk claimed that all of Oregon was American territory, and had used the campaign slogan "54-40 or Fight!" Once in the White House, he agreed to compromise at the 49th parallel.

Because most American settlers and employees of the Hudson's Bay Company anticipated that the border would extend west at the 49th parallel to the Columbia River then follow that river to the sea, the area that is now Western Washington was a no man's land that attracted only a handful of Americans. But in 1846, this became U.S. territory. Soon, a few pioneering families came to inspect the region and word soon passed among the pioneers that here was a magnificent land on the shores of a great inland sea. Migrants began moving north from the Willamette Valley.

The major problem for them was the isolation of the area. Northern Oregon was a great distance from the seat of government at Oregon City. Before long, residents north of the Columbia petitioned Congress to establish a new territory in this far northwest corner of the country. In 1853, Congress agreed and Washington Territory was born.

By the early 1880s, Seattle's population was approaching 4,000 and coal from mines east and south of Lake Washington had become a major export. This view of Seattle from atop Beacon Hill shows how the tide flats extended around the peninsula where Pioneer Square is located today. On the left are the Oregon Improvement Company coal docks at the foot of Jackson Street.

Three Mercer brothers made history in Seattle. Thomas arrived first and took a land claim at the foot of Queen Anne Hill. Aaron Mercer was the first settler to move his family east of Lake Washington. The youngest brother, Asa, shown here, was named "principal" or "president" of the University of Washington.

In the early 1880s, land in Eastern Washington that had been considered fit only for grazing was discovered to be ideal for growing wheat. The Palouse and Southwest Washington rapidly became major grain producers.

Soon after, irrigation waters made former desert lands blossom in the Yakima and Kittitas valleys. Dairies developed in the lush valleys of Western Washington. The Carnation Company, founded in Kent, was the most famous.

The fondest dreams of the pioneers were coming true in the 1880s. Population growth, slow at first, developed incrementally: from 11,594 in 1860 to 75,116 in 1880, 357,232 in 1890, 1,141,990 in 1910, 2,378,963 in 1950 and 4,132,204 by 1980. As the number of residents escalated, so did demand for services—legal, medical, educational, recreational and many others.

In the late 1800s, a wave of progress swept through Washington Territory. Increasing commerce sailed into Puget Sound beneath billowing canvas wings. Rivers, lakes and inland seas echoed with the snort of steam-driven craft. Manufacturers lit a hundred new furnaces and switched on a thousand new machines to produce goods for a

growing number of customers. Homes spread over once-forested hills; new schoolhouses were erected and old ones enlarged.

The basic catalyst for change was the railroad, which broke the isolation of the area. By 1886, about 900 miles of track laced through the Territory, more than half of it belonging to the Northern Pacific. On July 4, 1887, the first overland train arrived in Tacoma directly from Duluth. A year later, the Stampede Pass tunnel opened, replacing the steep switchbacked track over the summit. For the first time, the Northwest corner was firmly tied to the rest of the country.

In addition to lumber, coal and cattle, the Northern Pacific shipped east more than 4,000 tons of wheat in 1887 and 1,600 tons of other grains. That same year, ships on Puget Sound loaded 1,240,499 tons of Washington products for Pacific Rim trade. By 1889, the year of statehood, Washington exports had reached a value of close to $3 million. This

Puget Sound's magnificent waters were enjoyed by pioneer yachtsmen as early as 1875. The first Seattle Yacht Club was formed in 1879. By the time of this 1885 photo, yacht races were held annually on Elliott Bay, which also served as Henry Yesler's log pond.

The view west down Mill Street (Yesler Way) shortly after the Civil War shows the Occidental Hotel on the right with the high fir flagpole standing at the juncture of First, James and Mill. In the distance rises the smokestack of Yesler's sawmill.

When the proposed state constitution was placed before the voters, they approved it overwhelmingly. On the same ballot they voted to keep the capital in Olympia, and handily refused to sanction women's suffrage and prohibition (only men were voting, remember).

To legislate for the new state, the voters brought in a heavy preponderance of Republican legislators. Henry Drum of Pierce

included more than eight million pounds of hops, nearly a million tons of coal and 775 million board feet of lumber. The salmon pack was 205,000 cases, each case containing 48 one-pound cans.

On February 22, 1889, Congress passed enabling legislation and the clock began ticking toward statehood for Washington. On July 4, 1889, a constitutional convention convened in Olympia, consisting of 75 men, among them businessmen, lawyers, farmers, doctors, schoolteachers and ministers. The manager of the Tacoma Real Estate and Stock Exchange, Gwin Hicks, was the youngest delegate at age 32. Others included Yakima County developer William F. Prosser, Aberdeen lumberman A.J. West, Vancouver banker Lewis Johns, Spokane publisher Frank M. Dallam and Olympia engineer Thomas M. Reed.

One of the important subjects discussed at the convention was the question of the increasing power of corporations, especially railroad companies. One reaction against undue railroad influence was the inclusion of a law prohibiting free rail passes for elected officials. The question of tideflat properties was also a hot topic, with the majority of delegates favoring state control of such property except those acres legitimately claimed by settlers.

As the territorial days waned, several large mansions were built by wealthy businessmen on the slopes above the town. One of the finest was the home of James McNaught, by then famous as a railroad and corporation lawyer.

County was the single Democrat among the 35 senators. Only six Democrats were elected among the 70 representatives. Republicans took every state office, including the governor's chair, which was filled by former territorial governor Elisha P. Ferry.

On November 18, 1889, the elected officials and a crowd of about 3,000 gathered before the small frame statehouse in Olympia for the inaugural ceremonies. Immediately afterward, the elected leaders lost little time in getting to work. They and the citizens of the state embarked on the tremendous task of establishing a firm foundation upon which to develop the great 42nd state in the Union.

Dexter Horton's bank and the adjacent grocery store were gutted by the furious fire of 1889. The vault in the back of the bank preserved valuables and currency, however. Seafirst traces its roots to this little bank.

Ferry's Inaugural Speech

Elisha P. Ferry

In his inaugural address on November 18, 1889, Elisha P. Ferry, the first governor of the State of Washington, spoke of the new responsibilities of citizens.

"The substitution of a State Government for that of the Territory imposes on the citizens of Washington more solemn duties and graver responsibilities than those to which they have been accustomed. Hitherto the power of our Legislature to enact laws has been limited and restricted by the organic act and the amendments thereto and by the various laws that have been passed by Congress relating to the territories. Further than this, Congress reserved the right to annul any law passed by the territorial legislatures which seemed to be unwise and injudicious. We had no voice in the selecting of our executive and judicial offices and none in directing the course of the National Government.

"Hereafter all will be changed. The powers of our Legislature will be limited only by the Constitution of the United States and of the State of Washington. Our citizens will be on an equality with those of any other state of the Union and their wishes will have due weight in determining the policy of the National Government. We should, therefore, exercise a conscientious endeavor to bear well these new responsibilities and discharge faithfully the new duties which are ours and prove ourselves worthy of the rights which we have secured. Let greater wisdom accompany the greater power which we now possess."

Governor Ferry served two terms as territorial governor (1872-1880). He then resumed the practice of law in Seattle, where he was a member of one of the most prominent law firms in the Pacific Northwest— McNaught, Ferry, McNaught and Mitchell. He was also involved with several businesses, including Puget Sound National Bank, where he served as vice president. In 1889, Washington voters elected him the first state governor, for a term that ended in 1893. He lived in quiet retirement thereafter until his death in 1895 at age 70.

The Seattle waterfront was a jumble of wooden structures in 1889 before the June 6 fire and before statehood was granted in November. George Frye's brick Opera House on the southeast corner of Front and Marion bulks above the YMCA building and Budlong's Boat House, which served as the first yacht club.

The area burned by the great fire of 1889 stretches over what was the business section of Seattle. The photo, taken from the site where Harborview Hospital is today, shows the first tents that were erected. Scores of businesses operated under canvas until permanent quarters were erected of non-combustible materials.

The Burgeoning Years— 1890-1910

The new state of Washington came of age during the two decades that met at the turn of the century. The growing population provided expanding markets for manufacturers, farmers and professionals. In addition, the machines of the industrial revolution were moving west on ribbons of steel to this far northwest corner of America. Those same railroads also transported the products and goods of the state to eastern markets.

Growth and change did not begin in 1890, however. All through the previous decade, development had accelerated, especially after the transcontinental rails arrived in the mid-1880s. The railroads delivered increasing numbers of new residents to Washington, the majority finding employment in the cities, although farm families also increased in number. Except for a few suburbs that incorporated after World War II (Bellevue, for example),

By the turn of the century, Seattle was one of the fastest growing cities in the world. Pike Street, once far north of town, became a major commercial thoroughfare.

City (year incorporated)	1890 population	1910 population
Seattle (1865)	42,837	237,194
Spokane (1881)	19,922	104,402
Tacoma (1875)	36,006	83,743
Everett (1893)	—	24,814
Bellingham (1903)	—	24,298
Olympia (1859)	4,638	6,996
State of Washington	357,232	1,141,990

Top: *In 1893, Isaac Cooper and his brother-in-law Louis Levy opened a grocery and hardware store near the corner of First South and Yesler. A deep recession began to strangle commerce that year, but Cooper and Levy managed to hang on until 1897, when the ship* Portland *arrived with its ton of gold from the Klondike.*
Above: *On July 18, 1899, the steamer* Roanoke *arrived in Seattle with some proud sourdoughs aboard. Those bound wooden boxes contain nearly $4 million in gold.*

the urban areas of Washington State were formed by 1910, and began to dominate, as the population statistics on the previous page indicate.

Amidst the growth, a major recession took root in 1893, causing many new arrivals to suffer hardships before finding work. State and local governments were not anxious to assist these newcomers. What little assistance was available came from private agencies.

The antagonism between old residents and new is reflected in the aftermath of the 1889 fire that destroyed the heart of Seattle. Men flocked to town, expecting to find work rebuilding the burned area. But soon newspapers carried notices that no additional labor was needed. The unemployed newcomers were called "vagrants" in the press and urged to move on. After 1897, the recession was diluted by the effects of the

Before many autos were on the streets, accidents were already frequent.

Alaska Gold Rush, which immediately affected commercial interests of all kinds and which attracted still more people to the area.

This was also the era of new technical wonders. One was the automobile, which quickly changed the fabric of Northwest society. The first motor car appeared in the state in 1900. Six years later, 763 cars were chugging along state roads. In 1904, the Seattle City Council passed an ordinance requiring autos to have warning bells, gongs or whistles and established a speed limit of four mph downhill and eight mph uphill. The state began licensing vehicles in 1909, although the first license plates were not issued until 1915.

Along with the auto came electricity. The Tacoma Mill Co. installed electric lights in 1882; it was the first company in the area to do so. By 1910, this new power was lighting many urban homes and factories. Newly perfected electric motors were powering various machines, including streetcars and fans.

Technological improvements affected all businesses. For example, band saws and logging railroads increased efficiency in lumber manufacturing. By 1905, with the number of mills still rising, Washington was the leading lumber producing state, a distinc-

tion it carried for 30 years before being overtaken by Oregon. In 1903, the state passed the first laws to protect forests from fire.

Farmers also benefited from technology. New equipment and new crops were heralded every year. Between 1890 and 1910, Washington became a major agricultural producer. An agricultural college, now Washington State University, was founded in Pullman in 1892.

The first shipment of Washington apples went east by rail in 1894. Irrigation resulted in a million-bushel apple crop in 1895. By 1910, six million bushels were being produced annually.

Inland Empire wheat produc-

16

Seattle's First World's Fair

The Seattle business community hoped to mark the 10th anniversary of the 1897 discovery of gold in Alaska with a major event. The year was to be 1907, but plans were delayed. The Jamestown Exposition was already scheduled in Norfolk, Virginia for 1907 and it had sanction as a world's fair. Furthermore, a widespread financial downturn hit the country in 1907. The promoters managed to break ground for the event in June 1907, but rescheduled it for 1909.

The concept for the fair originated with Godfrey Chelander, who had organized a small Alaska exhibit at the 1905 Lewis and Clark Exposition in Portland and disliked the thought of disassembling his show. He thought Seattle might be interested in the display. Chelander had lived in Alaska for a number of years and was grand secretary of the Arctic Brotherhood.

Chelander made an appointment to meet with William Sheffield, secretary of the Alaska Club (later the Arctic Club), and the two discussed the possibilty of a permanant Alaskan exhibit in Seattle. Sheffield took Chelander to see James A. Wood, city editor of *The Seattle Times*, who liked

This view of the AYPE fairgrounds was taken from a window of the government building. The exposition monument rises in the foreground. The fair resulted in a few permanent buildings for the University of Washington, including the original Meany Hall.

the idea. The three men decided to interview the most influential of Seattle's business and professional leaders. They found almost unanimous support.

By 1906, the idea had turned into a major project. Articles of incorporation were filed and all local newspapers helped to publicize the event. The problem of a site was solved when Professor Edmond Meany suggested the University of Washington campus, still a largely forested area on the shores of Lake Washington. By holding the fair there, much of the university campus would be cleared and several exposition buildings could later be used by the university.

At first, promoters called the event the Alaska Exposition, but the plan was enlarged to include the Yukon Territory. Meany suggested that all countries bordering on the North Pacific be invited to participate. Emissaries fanned out around the Pacific— China, Japan, Hawaii, California and Canada. Eventually, all coastal states and many Pacific Rim nations agreed to provide exhibits. The name became the Alaska-Yukon-Pacific Exposition.

King County commissioners agreed to erect a $300,000 forestry building and to fund a $78,000 exhibit that would include a reproduction of the Newcastle coal mine and other Seattle area scenes in miniature.

The U.S. Congress provided $600,000 and Seattle citizens raised $1 million. Will H. Parry led the fundraising campaign, which met its goal by selling all the necessary stock to local business and industry leaders by June 1908.

The university campus was transformed into a beautiful park planned by the Olmsted brothers. About 20 buildings were erected to house activities and exhibits. The amusement section, "Pay Streak," fashioned after Chicago's

The 1909 fair attracted many famous orators, including William Jennings Bryan. A leading Democrat and advocate of the common man, Bryan had lost his third attempt for the presidency the previous year.

"Midway," entertained the multitudes.

June 1, 1909, the opening day, was declared a city holiday by Seattle Mayor John F. Miller. At 10 a.m., President William Howard Taft, at the nation's capital, pressed an Alaskan gold-nugget telegraph key, sending a signal across the country. More than 80,000 spectators cheered as the fair was opened.

The Exposition closed on October 16, 1908, free of debt. During its 138-day run, attendance reached a total of 3,740,551. Paid admissions totaled more than $1 million. The fair had achieved its major goals: to show the people of the world the enormous value of Alaska and the greatness of its main entry port, Seattle.

After the fair closed, the Seattle Chamber of Commerce hosted a banquet to salute the hardworking volunteers who had made the world's fair a success. W.A. Peters, a Seattle lawyer, praised them with these words: "Such men are the proudest possession of any community and the surest guaranty of its prosperity and greatness. Thus may your children's children, and generations on the heel of these, made mindful of our measure of your worth, themselves add honor to a noble heritage."

Those children's children would do just that at the Century 21 World's Fair of 1962.

Denny Hall on the new University of Washington campus was named after longtime university supporter and Seattle founder Arthur Armstrong Denny. This structure sheltered the entire university— laboratories, classrooms, bookstore, administration offices, professors' studies, music room, lecture hall and an assembly hall that seated 736.

tion escalated during these years as farmers discovered dry land wheat farming. The 1900 total of 1.3 million acres in wheat had doubled by 1910.

The number of dairy cows jumped from 119,000 in 1900 to 186,000 just 10 years later, and the state became self-sufficient in dairy products for the first time in 1912. By 1910, state hens were laying more than 14 million dozen eggs a year.

During this period, with Populism a strong political movement, farm cooperatives of various kinds blossomed.

By 1890, foundry and metalwork, brewing, wood finishing and printing were listed along with the extractive industries as major employers. Between 1890 and 1910, meat packing and general manufacturing increased markedly. The value of goods manufactured in the state exceeded $70 million by 1900.

Alaskan gold sprinkled the state after 1897, helping to underwrite manufacturing and retailing establishments that supplied Alaskan markets and other Pacific Rim customers. Values of Washington-produced clay, metal, bakery products and beer increased more than 600 percent during the two decades. Manufacturing payrolls rose from $12.6 million in 1890 to $59.6 million in 1910.

The new age was also demanding better educated workers. In 1895, the "Barefoot Schoolboy Law" was enacted to equalize public school funding throughout the state. During this period, many high schools opened, including Broadway (1902) and Lincoln (1909) in Seattle and Stadium (1906) in Tacoma. Central, Eastern and Western Washington State Universities were founded during the 1890s as normal schools to train needed teachers. Several private colleges also opened.

Financial services developed strongly during those years, although about half of the 173 banks in the state either failed, liquidated or merged during the recession of the 1890s. In 1907,

In 1892, the first city park superintendent was appointed. In 1903, the park board commissioned John C. Olmsted of Olmsted Brothers Landscape Architects to recommend a system for park extension and improvement. Several parks by then were already included in the Seattle system, including Lincoln Park at 10th and Pine, which was a popular place to swing.

Before the floating bridges, steamers such as the Fortuna *were the major means of transporting both passengers and freight to communities around Lake Washington.*

however, 192 state, 45 national and 70 private banks were counted. That year, a state banking department was created.

Those years also witnessed many advancements in medicine, engineering, legal and other services.

As the number of well-to-do families with spare time increased, recreation became a major industry. Formal leagues for baseball and football were formed and tennis, golf and yachting groups were organized. Libraries were built in every town, including Seattle, which was aided by Andrew Carnegie's gift of $200,000. In 1903, the Seattle Symphony played its first concert and other arts groups were active. As the decade drew to a close, the 1909 Alaska-Yukon-Pacific Exposition focused attention on Washington State as a developing international trading center.

Roaring Guns, Roaring Twenties—1911-1930

The volatile decades between 1911 and 1930 are marked in our history by World War I and the Roaring Twenties. During those years, Americans changed the way they traveled, the way they worked and the way they played. In turn, these changes spawned dozens of new business opportunities, altered the American lifestyle and changed urban skylines. The Seattle of 1930 (population 365,583) bore little resemblance to the city of 1911 (population 237,194).

Transportation modes were altered drastically. By 1920, the internal combustion engine was taking over the short haul business. With the mass-produced Model T Ford selling for as little as $400, Americans began to consider cars a necessity.

Trucks and buses joined the family flivver on the highway. In 1921, the year the state established a department of licensing, the vehicle count was 195,074, including 27,757 trucks, 929 stages (buses) and 798 trailers.

The government had to figure out a way to pay for construction of highways, roads and streets. One solution was a state gasoline tax of one cent per gallon, enacted in 1921.

Many small-time entrepreneurs founded local transportation companies. Starting in 1921, when the state began requiring reliable schedules and certification of vehicle maintenance, better financed companies took over most routes. Auto dealers, garages, service stations, auto camps (motels), parts stores and repair facilities also proliferated.

In 1910, Tacomans voted to build a municipal dock and the following year King County citizens formed the Port of Seattle district. In 1917, the Lake Washington Ship Canal opened, permitting large ships into Lake Union and Lake Washington.

In 1924, Ezra Meeker, age 94, flew from Seattle to Dayton, Ohio in three days, following the route that 72 years earlier had taken him seven months to travel by covered wagon.

In 1927, after his historic solo flight across the Atlantic, Charles Lindbergh toured the country to promote airfield construction. Soon after his "Spirit of St. Louis" landed at Sand Point, King County began building Boeing Field.

During the Great War, contracts were signed with many local industries. By 1917, Seattle shipbuilders were setting production records, first for wooden and later for steel ships. Pierce County residents purchased several thousand acres of prairie land and

In 1924 the 12-story Olympic Hotel was under construction and would open the next year. Its two wings were erected around the Metropolitan Theater (lower left), which was demolished in 1958 to make way for a "carriage entrance" for the hotel.

Above: *Pioneer Place during the years of the First World War was a grassed and fenced enclosure. The original totem pole, later destroyed by fire and dry rot, stands proudly.*

Upper inset: *Mrs. John W. Eddy (Ethel Garrett) invited some friends to a garden party at her Boylston Avenue home in 1924. Her husband, an 1895 Harvard graduate, made a fortune in the lumber industry in Michigan and on Puget Sound.*

Lower inset: *Enoch Bagshaw (left) was U.W. football coach from 1921 to 1929. Of the several outstanding football players of his era, probably the most famous was George Wilson, the All-American halfback, shown on the right in this 1929 photo.*

gave it to Uncle Sam as a site for an army base. "Camp" Lewis was the result.

Existing military facilities, including Fort Lawton and the Bremerton Navy Yard, were also busy. Most of the spruce lumber for the manufacture of army aircraft came from Washington forests. Since that time, Washington has been a leading recipient of military dollars.

Between 1911 and 1930, electricity usage increased tremendously. During those years, most home appliances were electrified, including kitchen ranges, water heaters, refrigerators, mixers, toasters and phonographs. So were tools of the trades.

Soon, hydroelectric dams backed up huge storage lakes all across the state. Among them were dams on the White River (1910), the Elwha River (1912) and the Skagit River (1918). In 1929, the Army Corps of Engineers approved the Grand Coulee Dam project and the Columbia Basin irrigation-power plant.

In the late 1920s, two advances in the field of mass communication startled Northwesterners. The miracle of radio fed entertainment and information into Northwest homes. And at local movie theaters, sound was added to the pictures. Both developments created new business opportunities.

By 1915, the Smith Tower and other steel-ribbed skyscrapers altered our city skyline. Machines laid ribbons of macadam across the state and lengthy bridges arched across rivers where ferries once ran.

But the Roaring '20s didn't actually roar in Washington State.

The Dutch-owned Shell Oil Company delivered its first gasoline in the U.S. to Puget Sound service stations in 1912. The original deliveries in the Seattle area were carried in horse-drawn tanks. A few years later, the company was using hard-tired gasoline-driven trucks such as this one.

World War I resulted in many contracts for local shipyards. By 1918, seven Seattle yards were busy building both wooden and steel ships. When the war suddenly ended in 1919, work on most projects quickly halted. Unfinished and surplus ships were anchored in rows on Lake Union and in other quiet waters around Puget Sound.

The Montlake was the last of the original cross-canal bridges to be built. The Ballard, Fremont and University bridges were built between 1917 and 1919. At the time, there was little demand for a fourth bridge. But after the University of Washington football stadium was built in 1920, home game Saturdays resulted in traffic jams. So in 1925 the city completed the Montlake bridge.

Bertha Knight Landes took over as Seattle's mayor in 1926, the first women to be elected to lead a major U.S. city. Mayor Landes believed in strict law enforcement, sound management of City Light, a profitable street car system, improved traffic safety, enhanced park programs, and appointments based on merit. She was defeated after serving one two-year term.

From 1915 to 1939, garbage disposal was the responsibility of the Seattle Health and Sanitation Department. This 1915 photo shows one crew at work.

In many ways, it was a troubled decade. The Harding era scandals resulted in a loss of trust in government leadership. During prohibition, which went into effect in our state in 1916, many otherwise good citizens disobeyed the law. Older and more conservative people were shocked by women's skimpy fashions, jazz music and other fads.

The 1920s was a time of shallow objectives. For many, pursuit of the almighty dollar ranked higher than ethics. Speculation sent prices of land and stocks and bonds ever higher. "Good times are here to stay" was a slogan of the time. Many believed it.

But on October 23, 1929, panic struck Wall Street. Stock values tumbled $5 billion that day. Losses on October 28 totaled $10 billion. Tens of thousands of investors watched helplessly as their fortunes vanished. The economic torture of the Great Depression had begun. Washington State would feel more than its share of pain in the next decade.

The Depression and The War Years—1931-1945

Old-timers vividly remember the 15 years between 1930 and 1945, when they rode an emotional and financial seesaw from peaceful plenty to depression-era hunger to wartime wages. During those lean depression years, living standards plummeted and the foundation of our political, social and economic life shook.

During the 1920s, almost everyone, including our country's presidents, predicted that prosperity was here to stay. The average family took on considerable debt, and businessmen used borrowed funds to build factories to meet soaring consumer demands. The stock market reflected the speculative fever.

After the weak financial foundation crumbled in October 1929, money was scarce. Debts went unpaid. Retail purchasing fell sharply. Factories and farms, unable to sell what they produced, reduced their work forces. Business spiraled downward as unemployment increased.

By 1933, nearly one-third of all American breadwinners were jobless. In Washington State, more than 287,000 men, women and children in need of food, clothing, shelter and medical care sought relief. Welfare was considered a problem of local governments, but their funds were soon depleted.

The table on the next page compares the years 1929 and 1933 and illustrates the rapid decline of industrial activity in the state.

Agriculture suffered less than

During the World War II years of 1943-5, Seattle's population increased by 112,000 as war workers flocked to town. Any day with some patriotic significance brought out military bands and marching units, as well as lots of red, white and blue bunting. Here such a parade marches up Seattle's Second Avenue.

industry because a drought had turned mid-America into a dust bowl. Local crops found ready markets, but at sharply reduced prices. Between 1929 and 1935, the farm population increased by 30,000 as the unemployed returned to the land in an effort to regain self- sufficiency. Still, lenders foreclosed on many farm mortgages and crop prices continued to drop. Between 1932 and 1936, farm income totaled only two-thirds of the 1927-31 income.

In 1932, because of the tightening grip of recession and the slowness of governmental reaction, the long dominant Republi-

Industry	Annual gross sales	
	1929	1933
Lumber	$263 million	$84 million
Flour milling	45 million	20 million
Meat packing	34 million	16 million
Printing/publishing	28 million	14 million
Fruit/vegetable canning	22 million	12 million
All industry	796 million	331 million
Other:		
Number of factories	4,648	2,307
Number of workers	114,635	67,752
Amount of wages	$160 million	$62 million

Much of the University of Washington campus was open space in 1939. At mid-picture is the golf course, present site of the medical school and football parking areas. To the right are the swampy edges of Lake Union that became a sanitary garbage fill and later a parking area and site of the horticulture school.

All during the war years, paper, metals, rubber and other materials were carefully recycled. This aluminum scrap, donated by citizens, was collected in a bin on University Street in front of the Olympic Hotel, a site called Victory Square.

can Party was swept from office all across the country. President Franklin D. Roosevelt and a new Congress acted swiftly to undergird failing banks. Deposits in Washington banks had fallen from $448 million to $212 million before the federal rescue.

Federal and state funds were channeled into programs to hire the unemployed. Counties, cities and private individuals contributed their share. These were not give-away programs. Results are obvious half a century later in scores of public buildings, air fields, bridges (the first Lake Washington floating bridge was built partly with funds from the Works Progress Administration), highways, park trails and accommodations—the list is long. In 1934-35, investments in such projects in Washington totaled $50 million. Federal funds were used to reclaim the Columbia Basin and

build the Grand Coulee and Bonneville dams. These projects involved many private companies. Grand Coulee, for example, used four million barrels of concrete

July 4, 1944 found Seattleites of all ages enjoying a major parade.

produced by six Washington State plants employing 1,200 men. Federal dollars were loaned to businesses by the Reconstruction Finance Corporation and to banks through the Federal Home Loan Bank Board. The Agricultural Adjustment Administration and Farm Credit Administration distributed federal largesse to farmers.

Expenses of state government soared as funds were raised to match federal dollars. The state budget reached $65 million in 1936, three times the 1920 budget. Legislation was passed authorizing a two percent sales tax to help meet costs. Although many Washingtonians questioned the large increase in government spending, the vast majority voted to re-elect the Democrats in 1936.

In the mid-1930s, after Hitler began his sinister moves in Europe, the United States decided to rearm. Washington companies were among the first to profit. By the time the Japanese attacked Pearl Harbor on December 7, 1941, contracts worth more than $1.5 billion had been assigned to local firms. By the end of the war, this had grown to $6 billion.

The need for workers in the expanding defense industry attracted 300,000 new residents to Washington, most of them to the Seattle area. Wages in the state's manufacturing industries rose from $32 million in 1939 to $550 million in 1945. Washington farmers were busy as well, producing foodstuffs for the armed forces, our allies and the home front. Wheat production, for example, jumped from 29 million bushels in 1939 to 78 million bushels in 1945.

Shipbuilding accounted for almost half of all wartime industrial activity in the state. The Boeing Company was busy building B-17s, the first of which rolled off the line in 1938, and later B-29s. Most major companies were busy in the war effort.

In Eastern Washington, a mystery town—Richland—arose almost overnight. Only after the first atom bomb fell on Japan did we learn what was going on there. The Army forts—Lewis, Wright, Flagler, Worden and Lawton, were busy, as was the Seattle waterfront, which operated as a Port of Embarkation. The Navy repaired battle-damaged ships at its Bremerton yard and operated Keyport Torpedo Station, Bangor Ammunition Depot, Pier 91, and the Sand Point and Whidbey Island air fields. The Army Air Force flew out of McChord, Paine, Larson, Geiger and Fairchild air fields.

Most importantly, we cannot forget the more than 200,000 Washington sons and daughters who served in the armed services, and especially the 5,414 who gave their lives during the war.

Construction of Grand Coulee Dam began in 1933 and was completed in 1942. By October 1941, the first generators were sending electricity along the lines. This timely construction provided badly needed electricity for the war effort.

On March 29, 1942, 15 army trucks arrived on Bainbridge Island. They dispersed to the homes of nearly 200 residents of Japanese ancestry, loaded them aboard, and carried them to Seattle, the first step toward California and Idaho detention camps. Under Executive Order 9066, all persons of Japanese ancestry, many of them U.S. citizens, were moved inland to these crude temporary quarters.

The Postwar Boom— 1946-1962

As World War II became history, the burgeoning Seattle population began to spread into the suburbs east of Lake Washington. In 1946, Kemper Freeman began building his Bellevue Shopping Square, shown here about two years after the first floating bridge opened.

The Second World War, historians say, was the last popular war. Americans did not doubt that they were battling evil enemies.

After V-J Day, the GIs flooded home to take advantage of the GI Bill, which paid for millions of them to attend college. GI loans allowed millions of them to purchase homes, and war surplus stores offered everything from olive drab underwear to surplus jeeps at a fraction of the original cost. Many a wedding was solemnized in the last half of the 1940s, and a baby boom soon followed.

Instead of the feared postwar recession, manufacturers struggled to meet consumer demand. After 10 years of the worst depression in history and five years of a wartime economy that paid good wages but directed production to the war effort, American families went on a buying spree. They replaced worn-out appliances and autos, repaired their homes or moved to better ones, and replenished their wardrobes with double-breasted suits and longer dresses now that wartime material shortages were history. They also purchased new products, the prime example being television sets. Seattle's first television station began broadcasting in 1947.

The aura of peace was soon shattered, however. The GIs were hardly through college when the Korean conflict flared up in 1950. The term "cold war" became part of our lexicon. Meanwhile, the Berlin land blockade had been overcome by American air carriers, we began rebuilding Europe under the Marshall Plan, NATO came into being and the U.S. was recognized as the strongest nation in the world.

The Russians stunned this country in 1957 by hoisting Sputnik into space. The United States responded with a surge of support for science education, sent the chimpanzee Ham into space in January 1961 and rocketed Alan Shepard skyward five months later. In 1962, John Glenn became the first American to orbit the earth.

Although most people enjoyed the pleasures of the good life and

Postwar auto dealers experienced prosperous times following 10 years of depression and five years of World War II. This futuristic Chevrolet on display at the 1957 auto show received many an admiring glance.

sensed that international conflicts were comparatively small and distant, discomforting portents of the future were in evidence. In 1954, we hardly noticed when the French were driven from Vietnam, but eight years later the U.S. was dispatching both aid and army units to assist the South Vietnamese in fighting Communist invad-

Governor Albert Rosellini spoke at the opening of the Evergreen Point Bridge in 1963. The structure would later be named for him.

The Century 21 World's Fair

Seattle's second world's fair was an even greater success than the first. The late Nard Jones, in his book *Seattle*, tells the story of how the fair concept was born. Four men—Don Follett and Denny Givens of the Seattle Chamber of Commerce, City Councilman Al Rochester and *Seattle Times* executive Ross Cunningham—discussed the fact that Seattle was in the post-war doldrums and needed a new focus. Cunningham had known some of the organizers of the Alaska-Yukon-Pacific Exposition of 1909 and he suggested that a world's fair might attract tourists and provide a badly needed cultural center for Seattle.

They discussed an exposition for the year 1959, a half century after the AYPE. Rochester promoted the concept with his fellow politicians. Jerry Hoeck and Marlow Hartung, both in the advertising business, came up with a title—the Century 21 Exposition. That seemed more and more appropriate as time went on, for the Russians sent Sputnik skyward and the United States was entering the Space Age, with the substantial involvement of The Boeing Company. The city council asked Governor Arthur Langlie to appoint a world's fair study commission. He named Edward Carlson as chairman.

The commission developed plans for "a fair in a jewel box." The Civic Center was the

This promotional picture for the Century 21 World's Fair was used before the fair buildings were completed. It superimposes a picture of a world's fair model onto a photo of the city.

This street of educational entertainment at the Seattle World's Fair was called Boulevard 21. It was the site of the pavilions of the General Electric Co., hydroelectric companies, railroad companies, natural gas companies and the Ford Co.

chosen site, with the hope that the fair would leave several permanent buildings there. Adjacent properties were purchased to enlarge the site to 74 acres, considered the minimum needed for a world's fair. Seattle voters passed a $7.5 million bond issue to support the fair. Albert D. Rosellini, who had assumed the governor's chair in Olympia, promised that the state would match the amount raised by Seattle. Of the $7.5 million in state funding, $4.5 million was set aside for the Washington State exhibit and the Coliseum in which it would be housed.

Several hundred dedicated Seattle business leaders, civic leaders, public officials and citizen volunteers were involved in preparing for the grand extravaganza. The date continued to be a problem and was changed twice. Ewen Dingwall was named project director, then promoted to vice president and general manager. Jim Faber, public relations director, visited the Brussels exposition and on the way home stopped off in the office of powerful Senator Warren G. Magnuson. In the end, the U.S. government provided $12.5 million for the fair, including money for the Science Pavilion (now the Science Center).

Alweg of Sweden provided the plans and equipment for the monorail that would carry visitors the 1.2 miles from downtown Seattle to the fairgrounds.

In November 1960, the Bureau of International Expositions in France agreed that Century 21 should be sanctioned as a legitimate world's fair. Soon, the event was known in common parlance as the Seattle World's Fair.

Eddie Carlson, who had seen the revolving television tower in Stuttgart, conceived of a combination high-rise restaurant and observation platform. John Graham and Associates designed and the Howard S. Wright Company built the 600-foot Space Needle.

On April 21, 1962, at 12 noon Seattle time, President John F. Kennedy pressed the same gold nugget telegraph key that had opened the 1909 exposition. This time, instead of a direct telegraphic impulse by wire, the signal was run through a computer in Maine that focused a radio telescope on the star Cassiopeia A, some 60,000 billion-billion miles away. From that star, the telescope picked up a light vibration that had begun its journey about 10,000 years earlier and instantly relayed it to Seattle. The fair was officially open.

In six months, 10 million visitors attended the fair, contributing to the city's prosperity and learning about the promise of the future. As a legacy, the fair left several buildings in a permanent Seattle Center that attracts millions each year.

Group Health pioneered the prepaid comprehensive cooperative medical plan in the Puget Sound area. This group of founders met in 1947 to discuss ways in which the consumer-owned group could provide medical services. Since then, though much imitated, Group Health has remained the largest of such groups in the region.

ers. Nations in the Middle East were growing testy as the new state of Israel fought for the right to exist.

In this country, the Supreme Court unanimously ordered school integration in 1954. Two years later, black citizens boycotted the segregated Montgomery, Alabama bus system, and Dr. Martin Luther King, Jr. began his campaign of peaceful resistance against racial prejudice, for which he would be awarded the Nobel Peace Prize.

Here in the Northwest, the population jumped more than 40 percent during the 1940s. The war effort had attracted thousands of workers to the cities, and thousands of servicemen and women traveled through the area during the war years. Many of them decided to make their homes in the Northwest. The population of King County grew from 504,980 in 1940 to 732,992 in 1950.

Many new jobs were created. Leisure and sportswear designed and manufactured in the Northwest became popular; electronic and high-tech businesses were founded; medical supply companies, food industries, and lumber and building suppliers flourished. Puget Sound ports were busy shipping goods to Pacific Rim destinations.

In 1961, when President John F. Kennedy was on campus to help the University of Washington celebrate its centennial, he was faced with an array of signs calling for an end to nuclear testing and supporting his "race for peace." This was but the outset of the protest era.

Suburbia became a spreading phenomenon. Towns grew up around crossroad service stations. Bellevue, which incorporated in 1953, was home to nearly 13,000 by 1960 and 61,000 by 1970. Lynnwood, incorporated in 1959, counted 7,200 residents in 1960 and 17,000 in 1970. Mountlake Terrace, incorporated in 1954, was home to 9,100 in 1960 and 16,600 in 1970.

This increasing population required new highways and utility services. Metro came into being, and in 1958 King County citizens voted to spend $80 million on area-wide sewer projects that would allow our lakes, streams and Sound to cleanse themselves. To supply electric power, existing dams were enlarged and new ones were built. Other utili-ties scrambled to keep up with demand.

Colleges and universities continued to build new facilities to meet increasing enrollments. The demands on health services elicited new responses, such as the formation of Group Health Cooperative of Puget Sound, the first of many HMOs.

Growing numbers of air travelers increased the need not only for airplanes but airfields as well. The Port of Seattle dedicated Sea-Tac Airport in 1947. In 1954, The Boeing Airplane Company rolled out its model 707. This first jet passenger airliner would take the world by storm and make the Boeing name the most prominent among manufacturers of passenger aircraft.

Local activities sometimes reflected national and international events. The Cold War, in particular, resulted in some extreme reactions. For example, legislator Al Canwell of Spokane undertook an overzealous hunt for communists on the University of Washington campus and elsewhere. He was defeated in his 1948 re-election bid. Canwell's activities pre-dated by a few months the national rise of the infamous Senator Joseph McCarthy.

The era was crowned in 1962 by the Century 21 World's Fair, which attracted nearly 10 million visitors to Seattle and left a valuable legacy—the Seattle Center, with its opera house, coliseum, science center and other structures. Although it is aging, the Seattle Center is still heavily used to this day.

Protests and Progress— 1963-1974

In the 1960s, citizens all across the country became restive over governmental resistance to change. Seattle and the State of Washington did not escape this trend.

On the local scene, the decade of protest began when a group called Citizens for Charter Reform stirred up the political porridge. As a result, in the 1967 elections, three new and younger candidates—Phyllis Lamphere, Tim Hill and Sam Smith—replaced older members of the Seattle City Council. Soon after, CHECC (Choose An Effective City Council) generated more heat

In March 1963, the Evergreen Point Bridge was being built across Lake Washington toward the eastern shore. It would open on August 18 as a toll bridge (35 cents per car). By June 1979, just 16 years later, the bonds had all been redeemed and the tolls were removed.

and George Cooley, John Miller and Bruce Chapman were added to the council.

County politicians also took their lumps. With more than 92 percent of King County residents living in urban areas, the Municipal League and League of Women Voters agitated for a more responsive form of government. As a result, a county executive and county council replaced the former county commissioners.

It was a time when development was tempered by preservation efforts. In 1965, architect Ralph Anderson moved his office into a grimy, three-story structure in Pioneer Square that was built in 1902. He renovated it and so began the preservation of that historic part of town.

Pike Place Market, with strong leadership from Victor Steinbrueck, was also saved and renovated, thanks to community activists. Today, the market is thriving as one of the city's key tourist attractions and a popular shopping spot for residents.

Daniel J. Evans was sworn in as governor in January 1965. He was the first governor to be elected to three consecutive terms. He would later serve as president of The Evergreen State College and as a Washington State senator.

As the population of the region increased, more autos squeezed onto inadequate highways. Major transportation construction projects marked this era. Interstate 5 reached through Seattle in 1967, and later Highway 405 was built around the east side of Lake Washington, in part to serve the new Boeing facilities at Paine Field. The Evergreen Point Bridge opened in 1963. After the R.H. Thomson throughway to the floating bridge had been partially built, neighborhood activists blocked completion of the roadway. To this day, near the Montlake interchange, concrete onramps soar skyward to nowhere.

The latter half of this era brought louder demands, longer protest marches and increasing youthful unrest. In the background was the growing unpopularity of the U.S. involvement in the Vietnam War. Black citizens continued pushing for equal opportunity; women sought equal rights. Thousands of chanting students marched down the new I-5 freeway from the University District

The 1960s were filled with protests against discrimination, the Vietnam War, nuclear arms and power plants, and many other developments. In 1962, a general student strike was called and students from colleges all across the state marched in a mammoth parade down I-5 to downtown Seattle. Here University of Washington students are shown rallying before the march.

The Pike Place Market

There was a time when King County farmers hawked their produce door to door or turned it over to wholesalers who paid them a percentage of the selling price. Usually, if the produce wilted, the farmers took the loss.

In 1906, fresh produce prices rose steeply along with other prices. The inflation was partly the result of the demand for Northwest lumber and produce in San Francisco as it rebuilt after the great earthquake. Local customers accused the middlemen of collusion.

A reform-minded city councilman, Thomas P. Revelle, came across an 1896 Seattle ordinance authorizing a public market. Knowing the Street Department had recently finished planking Western Avenue at the end of Pike Street, he and fellow coun-

The modern Pike Place Market attracts both residents and visitors to its colorful stalls of produce and its unusual stores and restaurants.

cilmen passed legislation on August 5, 1907 creating the Pike Place Public Market. It was an immediate success.

Now Frank Goodwin and his brothers John and Ervin enter the picture. They had returned from the Alaskan gold rush with $50,000 in gold dust. They in-

vested in property, including the bluff to the west of the end of Pike Street. They became aware of the crowds of shoppers buying farm produce from the wagons. Even on rainy days, business boomed. Goodwin figured that a sheltered shed on the bluff they owned might be rentable to these farmers. He sketched a plan for this shelter, extending it north from the Leland Hotel, which he owned. The plan was revised to include 76 covered stalls that could be rented for $4 to $25 per month. The building was completed in November 1907.

By 1910, the city was building adjoining arcades, which extended from Pike to Stewart Streets. In 1911, Seattle created an office of Market Inspector to maintain the quality of produce. In 1913, a bond measure passed allowing the stalls to be improved and additional arcades built. The Goodwins, meanwhile, with private capital, added the Public Market Building and additions, providing space for 100 shops.

During the First World War, the market was a busy place. It would experience many fluctuations in business over the years, through times of private ownership, then back to public control.

In 1971, at the urging of "Friends of the Market" and leaders such as Victor Steinbrueck, voters created a seven-acre historical market district and a commission to oversee it. Since then, millions of dollars have been spent to refurbish and expand this uniquely popular and historic part of our city.

The Pike Place Market in 1912.

After the Lake Washington Ship Canal was completed, the Port of Seattle's Fishermen's Terminal became the major mooring site for the North Pacific fishing fleet.

to downtown Seattle. It seemed like everyone had a cause they felt deeply about. Seattle experienced minimal violence during this time, although militants bombed the homes of two state legislators, the U.W. ROTC building and a City Light substation.

A troublesome recession dogged the Pacific Northwest from 1970-72, reflecting the troubles at The Boeing Company. Air travel had not increased as rapidly as predicted and the government canceled its contract for the supersonic prototype under development at Boeing. The company was forced to reduce its work force by about two-thirds, or 65,000. Fewer than 15 percent of those laid off left Seattle, however. Most hung on until they could find another job in the area

or until they were rehired by Boeing. Some started their own businesses. At the nadir of the recession, unemployment in King County exceeded 12 percent.

Construction in downtown Seattle continued through these years at a record pace. More than three million square feet of office space became available in a dozen major buildings. The Port of Seattle modernized to the tune of $250 million. Among its additions were new containerized cargo facilities.

Attorney James Ellis led the Forward Thrust program for improved public facilities. In 1968, the public approved $313.9 million in local programs. This was the largest per capita public improvement plan ever approved in the United States. To this day, we

enjoy the results, including the Kingdome, nearly 5,000 acres of park land, 200 miles of improved arterials, an improved Youth Service Center, 13 new fire stations, neighborhood improvements and $70 million worth of sewers.

Between 1965 and 1975, the suburbs blossomed while Seattle's population fell by 55,000. During those 10 years, King County's population increased by 24 percent. Families followed businesses to the suburbs while in Seattle the number of one- and two-person domiciles increased sharply. All the picketing, rioting, shouting and planning resulted in many changes. As a result, the Seattle area became a better place in which to live. A relatively peaceful and prosperous era would follow.

Waning Inflation, Rising Skyline—1975-1989

As the 1970s waned, residents of the region hotly debated the nuclear energy question. Skagit County voters trooped to the polls to produce a strong "no nukes" advisory vote. At Satsop and Hanford, plant construction was halted or delayed. The Washington Public Power Supply System (WPPSS) slipped into default, leaving bondholders holding an empty bag.

Inflation and high interest rates carried over into the early 1980s. Between 1972 and 1987, the consumer price index rose 172 percent. The price of housing increased more than 200 percent. This slowed building construction, which in turn exacerbated the recession in the state's timber industry.

In 1980, Washington State's nine presidential electoral votes went to Ronald Reagan, who during his campaign had promised to control inflation, lower taxes, strengthen national defense and reduce the budget deficit.

Washington State lost its two powerful Democratic senators during the 1980s. An aging Warren G. Magnuson was defeated in 1981 by Slade Gorton, but the retired "Maggie" would remain a part of the political scene until his death in 1989. Senator Henry Jackson died suddenly in 1983 and former governor Daniel J. Evans was appointed to replace him. For the first time in more than four decades, both of the state's senators were not only Republicans, but first-termers.

The U.S. withdrawal from

A United flight rises skyward from Sea-Tac with the mighty mountain in the background.

Seattle's new skyline forms a backdrop for the Port of Seattle's container cargo facilities.

A night scene of mid-town Seattle.

Airborne Express takes off, bound for another speedy delivery.

Vietnam in 1975 triggered an influx of Southeast Asian refugees into the Puget Sound area. The vast majority of these hardworking immigrants soon found jobs and became self-supporting.

The skyline of Puget Sound cities sprouted heavenward during these years. The growth started in 1960 in Seattle with the Norton, Washington and Logan buildings—small structures compared to what followed. The 50-story Scafirst building bulkcd into thc sky in 1968-69, and was followed by such skyscrapers as the Bank of California, Park Place, the Federal Building, Unigard Financial Center, the Rainier Tower, the Telephone Building, the Seafirst Fifth Avenue Plaza and the tallest of them all, the Columbia Center. Additional towering structures are now under construction, including Pacific First Centre, Two University Square and the AT&T Gateway Tower.

All of this construction plus the excavation for the Metro bus tunnel made driving downtown difficult. The resulting congestion and other traffic problems no doubt influenced Seattle voters in 1989 to overwhelmingly approve a controversial plan to control the growth of downtown and the height of new buildings.

Meanwhile, the suburbs, too, began to develop highrise core cities, with Bellevue leading the way.

Business left positive tracks during much of the period, although the stock market tipped precipitously, falling 508 points on October 20, 1987 and causing ghosts of the Great Depression to haunt conversations. But the market recovered quickly.

The Puget Sound area developed further ties with Pacific Rim trading partners such as Japan, Canada, Taiwan, South Korea,

Bellevue, too, now has structures that rise high.

Singapore, Hong Kong and the Philippines. The People's Republic of China opened its doors wider and the Soviet Union came trading for Northwest grain.

The 1980s also brought further diversification of industry in this region. While The Boeing Company, the state's largest employer, developed a tremendous backlog of orders for its jetliners, other industries—machinery, fabricated metals, electronic equipment and computer software—increased in importance.

With the growth of industry came an upsurge in population that is predicted to continue, or even accelerate until the year 2000. Barring recessions and other catastrophes, before the turn of the century, the number of state residents, now approaching 4.5 million, may increase by another million, most of them in the Puget Sound region.

43

Seattle's Industries

The George E. Starr *was the first steamer built on the Seattle waterfront. J.F.T. Mitchell launched the 148-foot wooden sidewheeler in 1879.*

Inset upper left: *Cherry Creek and Cherry Valley cross the Snohomish and King County line where, by 1924, the lush pastures were supporting large dairy herds.*
Inset lower left: *Union Depot in 1920 was called the Oregon-Washington Station and served several different rail lines. All kinds of land transportation (even a bicycle and perambulator) are represented in the photo.*
Inset above: *This highly decorated brass and marble bank interior was the pride of Dexter Horton and Company in 1894. Note the spittoons.*

Overview

From its founding in 1889 in a false-front, one-story store, Frederick and Nelson advanced to this familiar structure at Fifth and Pine just 27 years later. D.E. Frederick and Nels Nelson were a compatible pair with Frederick managing and Nelson selling.

The inexorable movement of Americans to the Pacific Northwest has continued unabated for 150 years. Currently, business is generating new jobs in the area while California and other crowded areas are developing discomfort zones, so the influx of new residents to Washington is likely to increase even more rapidly in the years ahead.

The population mix is also changing. While the number of state residents increased 8.4 percent between 1980 to 1987, the white population grew only 6.5 percent. The Native American population increased 12.2 percent, the black population 16.6 percent, Asians and Pacific Islanders 34.4 percent and others, primarily Hispanics, 62.9 percent. Meanwhile, the average age of the population is also increasing, following a nationwide pattern.

King County, with nearly 1.4 million residents, is the 18th most populous county in the nation. It has more than twice the population of Pierce County, Washington's second most populous county. Of the almost 4.5 million Washingtonians, about one-third live in King County. Seattle, the largest city in the state and 24th largest in the United States, is surrounded on three sides by suburbs, seven of which rank among Washington's 25 largest cities.

In 1988, non-agricultural employment in the Seattle-Everett metropolitan area passed the one million mark. The expansion was due in large measure to The Boeing Company.

In January 1989, 1,007,300 were employed in non-agricultural jobs in King and Snohomish Counties, according to the State Department of Employment Security. Of these, 550,200 were in the fields of trade, finance and services, 206,000 in manufacturing and 251,100 in miscellaneous other fields.

The 1986 *Washington State Yearbook* lists the percentage of employees in each occupation group in King County as follows:

Occupation Group	Percent of Employment
Service industries	22.4%
Manufacturing	18.4
Retail trade	17.6
Government (local/state/federal)	13.7
Finance, insurance, real estate	8.2
Wholesale trade	7.4
Transportation and public utilities	6.6
Construction	4.9
Agriculture, forest products, fisheries and mining	0.9

Not long ago, this ranking was nearly reversed, with the natural resource industries and agriculture heading the list. In King County in particular, urbanization, automation and growth in services and manufacturing have drastically changed the employment picture over the last half century.

A list of the state's 10 leading industries in 1900 and in 1937 is shown at right. Note how little the proportions changed (except in the pulp and paper industry, in

The famed "Red Barn" was kept secure by army guards during World War I. The structure is now part of the Museum of Flight.

which new production methods were developed in the 1920s).

Today's employment trends indicate that Washington's service and retail industries will continue to grow and employ more people. The number of government employees has remained fairly steady. Statewide employment in durable and non-durable manufacturing has been declining because many of these jobs are being exported to Asia and Latin America. Non-manufacturing jobs in fields other than the service and retail trade are also decreasing steadily.

Of the thousands of businesses that exist today, several have histories going back a century or more. Service companies that meet a constant demand—such as funeral homes, law firms, banks and hospitals—are apt to have

Industry	1900	1937
1. Lumber and timber products	$31,665,000	$213,870,980
2. Pulp and paper	N.A.	91,341,357
3. Flour and grain products	6,774,000	50,324,629
4. Canning and preserving	5,090,000	31,217,908
5. Meat packing	4,293,953	29,769,628
6. Dairy products	1,190,000	25,223,824
7. Printing and publishing	1,975,000	22,035,320
8. Foundry, machine shop products	2,321,000	19,785,952
9. Bread and bakery products	654,000	19,292,065
10. Liquor	1,657,392	11,165,559
11. All others	15,637,392	161,639,770

This 1911 Nowell and Rognon photo is captioned: "Airship flights by Eugene B. Ely and Hugh Robinson on Elliott Bay." The event captured the attention of all the sailors.

longer histories than retail businesses.

The search for the oldest existing business in the Puget Sound area can be frustrating. Just when it appears the oldest has been found, an even older one surfaces. The *Post-Intelligencer,* which can trace its lineage to 1863, may be the oldest existing business in Seattle. Pope and Talbot of Port Gamble might be considered the oldest (1854) in the Puget Sound region or perhaps in the state.

Another interesting question: which major companies with national reputations were founded in the Seattle area? The Carnation Co. comes immediately to mind; its first condensery was in Kent. United Parcel Service first operated out of Pioneer Square on the site of the present Waterfall Park. The late Eddie Bauer began his businesses in Seattle. Nordstrom is now nationally known and is one of few retailers to remain in the same family through three generations. *The Seattle Times* is another business that has been operated by the same family for three generations. Pay 'n Save Drugs, Ernst Hardware and Lamonts are all chains that were founded and managed by M.L. Bean (they are now separately owned). Bartell Drugs, one of the oldest drug companies in the region, is still managed by the Bartell family. The list goes on.

Above: *William E. Boeing took up flying in 1914 and was convinced he could build a better "aeroplane." In 1916, the B and W was the first Boeing plane to fly. The company soon moved to an old boat yard on the Duwamish River which, by 1918, as the photo illustrates, had been enlarged.*

Inset above: *The Estep diesel manufactured by Washington Iron Works powered many Northwest ships. Here a large model is being installed on the ferry* Bainbridge.

Inset upper right: *Frederick Weyerhaeuser and partners purchased 900,000 acres of timberland in 1900 from the Northern Pacific Railroad. This was the largest single timber transaction in U.S. history, but not until World War I did the company produce large amounts of lumber.*

Aerospace

The history of the aerospace industry in Washington is largely the history of The Boeing Co. and its suppliers. In 1910, just 10 years after the Wright Brothers' plane took off over the sands of Kitty Hawk, Charles Hamilton flew the first plane in Seattle. It happened at the Meadows Race Track, now the site of the Boeing Field complex.

Six years after Hamilton soared above the crowd, William E. Boeing, the scion of a wealthy Minnesota timber and mining family who settled in Seattle, decided he could build a better airplane than those he had learned to fly. His first effort, the B and W, was assembled in a boathouse on Lake Union.

By the time the United States became enmeshed in the First World War, Boeing had a contract for 50 Model C trainers. The company had moved to a former boat building facility on the banks of the Duwamish River (the Red Barn, now preserved at the Museum of Flight).

Hard times followed the war, but in 1921 the tiny aerospace company received its first major postwar order, for 111 observation planes. Then, as now, The Boeing Co. employed outstanding engineers and craftsmen who developed new designs and improved old ones.

Boeing bid successfully on airmail contracts in the mid-1920s and by 1929 had developed one

of the largest aircraft plants in the country. After William Boeing took the firm public, he formed United Aircraft and Transport Corp., an umbrella for several profitable aerospace ventures.

The federal government took anti-trust action in 1934, however, and the corporation was forced to split into three independent companies. One remained The Boeing Co. and the other two became United Airlines and United Technologies. Shortly before the breakup, William Boeing, upset at the governmental decree, resigned from the company he had founded 17 years earlier.

During World War II, Boeing's B-17s and B-29s were famous around the world as the

The famous Boeing and Westervelt (B and W) was the first airplane built by The Boeing Company in a boathouse on Lake Union in 1916.

When the First Airplane Flew in Seattle

The "Bird Man" was what the local papers called Charles K. Hamilton, the first man to soar in Seattle's skies. Hamilton was one of America's first barnstormers. Under an arrangement with the Western Washington Fair Association, which sold several thousand tickets, Hamilton was to present a flying exhibition over a two-day period. His Glenn Curtis biplane was to lift off at the Meadows Racetrack, a major horse racing establishment located near the present Boeing Field.

The plane he flew was hardly more than a kite. The fragile fixed-wing bird was constructed of spruce and bamboo covered with rubberized silk, with a rudimentary engine mounted to face the rear behind the pilot. Hamilton must have been a true daredevil. He had just returned from the Far East, where he demonstrated dirigibles for Japanese military leaders.

Hamilton and his partner Al Crofton were now moving about the country with this exhibition. The Wright Brothers had first flown at Kitty Hawk, North Carolina, just seven years earlier. Most Americans had yet to witness manned flight; the novelty was a real drawing card.

A reporter in the crowd wrote of the event: ". . . the machine freed from its fetters and, as though alive, it caught itself against the element of its seeking and soared up and on until from a rapidly increasing momentum it ate up the distance above the course that used to throb with the pound

In 1910, Charles K. Hamilton soared above the crowd gathered at the Meadows Racetrack.

of flying horseflesh."

In an interview, Hamilton attempted to describe the thrill of flying. It was, he said: "a joy ride in an automobile without the bumps and without the continual apprehension of striking a street car or a tree. It brings with it a sensation that fills the aviator with a mania to be in the air and an exhilaration that cannot be equaled on earth."

But on that first day of the exhibition, Hamilton had a very bumpy ride. In fact, he almost killed himself. As he swooped down from 150 feet at about 40 miles an hour to skim the little lake in the center of the racetrack, he caught his wheels in the water and flipped his plane. The pond was about seven feet deep and the dazed Bird Man was in trouble until rescued by men in a rowboat.

Meanwhile, on shore, partner Al Crofton was assuring the anxious spectators that "a cold bath would not keep a man from flying when he jumps into the very jaws of death every day of the year."

Once the rescue boat nosed terra firma, Hamilton insisted that he could walk, stepped out of the boat and promptly fainted. He was back the next day, however, walking on a knee swollen to nearly twice its normal size. He also was suffering a bad cold, but tried his best to fulfill the contract to fly before the assembled multitudes. The problem was the plane. It had been severely damaged. For five hours Hamilton wired parts together, replaced other parts and did his utmost to repair the flying machine while the crowd watched patiently. He finally had to give up.

When the announcement was made that the show had to be cancelled because the plane needed major repairs, the crowd dashed madly to the ticket gate to receive refunds. The crush became so great that two women fainted and a little boy sprained his arm.

Nonetheless, history was made. Charles Hamilton had flown the first airplane in Seattle.

The Most Famous Airplane Built by Boeing

The Boeing Company's most famous airplane (with the possible exception of the 707 series of modern times) was the B-17, the forerunner of the larger B-29. The B-17 has even been called the most famous plane in history, although some would argue that the honor belongs to the Wright Brothers' first airplane at Kitty Hawk.

Design work on the B-17 began in 1934. Early in the process, in answer to the Army Air Force's request for a long-range bomber, Boeing engineers drew up plans for a four-engine plane rather than the standard two-engine model.

This Boeing model 299 out-performed its rivals even though during final tests an army pilot took off with controls locked, crashing the prototype. Nevertheless, the army ordered 13 test models under the designation B-17.

The experiences of the British Air Force during the early years of World War II resulted in major improvements in the B-17, including greater firepower, self-sealing tanks and heavier armor. It was during this time that the plane became known as the "flying fortress."

Many design changes were made to the B-17. For example, the model first distinguished by the enlarged tail and turrets in the tail, top and belly was known as the B-17E. These were the first U.S. Army Air Force bombers to drop their loads on Germany. The B-17G was the final model designation before production ended in April 1945.

At the peak of B-17 production in June 1944, the Seattle plant was rolling out 16 airplanes every 24 hours. In all, 12,725 B-17s came off the assembly lines, about two-thirds of them at Boeing plants, the remainder from Lockheed-Vega and Douglas.

Before the war, Boeing experimented with the B-17, pressurizing the cabin and improving performance in other ways. In 1940, when the army invited bids for a high-altitude, long-range bomber, the army ordered three Boeing Model 345s, or as the army numbered them, XB-29s.

When the first B-29 flew in September 1942, it was far ahead of its competitors in defense armament, pressurized components and engine design. The army ordered large-scale production even before the prototypes were completed. The Boeing plant in Wichita was enlarged and the Boeing Renton plant converted to produce B-29s. Bell and Martin were ordered to build B-29s in Marietta, Georgia and Omaha, Nebraska. By war's end, nearly 4,000 B-29s had rolled off the assembly lines.

It was the B-29 that first bombed Japan in June 1944, and B-29s dropped the two

Tail assemblies of the Boeing B-17 are lined up in the Seattle factory during World War II.

nuclear bombs on Japan that ended the war.

After the war, Boeing produced the B-50 Superfortress, a direct descendant of the B-29. In 1943, the company began developing a sweptwing jet bomber, the B-47, the first of which flew in 1947. This was followed by the B-52 Stratofortress, a direct descendant of the B-47.

During these years, Boeing was also producing new commercial models. Between 1947 and 1949, the company manufactured 56 of the Model 377 Stratocruisers.

In August 1952, Boeing president William Allen announced that the company would invest $16 million in the development of a new jet-powered transport. Engineers referred to the model as the "Dash Eighty," for model 367-80. Sales staff and the public soon called it the Model 707.

The first 707 flew in 1954. Since then, the 707 has become without doubt the most modified airplane in the world. The original prototype 367-80 was accepted by the Smithsonian Institution as one of the 12 most significant aircraft of all time.

The 727 followed in 1962, the 737 in 1967, the 747 in 1968, the 767 in 1981 and the 757 in 1982. Each new model was designed for a specific type of air service. The success of the 707 models is apparent. As of the end of June, 1989, Boeing held unfilled firm orders for 1,707 planes worth about $61 billion.

bombers that were winning the war. After the conflict, a down cycle hit the company. William E. Allen, the president (who followed Phil Johnson and Claire Egtvedt), realized that drastic action was required, and ordered work to commence on a commercial jetliner. From the 1954 prototype came the 727 in 1960, the 747 in 1966, and the 757 and 767 in the 1970s.

In 1958, Boeing won contracts to assemble and test the Minuteman missile. During the 1960s, it built lunar orbiters that photographed the moon, the first stage of the Saturn V moon rocket, a buggy that traveled on the moon's surface, and the first spacecraft to complete a two-planet mission. More recently, Boeing has helped develop the Stealth Bomber, an effort that engages 10,000 Boeing employees.

In the late 1960s, a fateful downturn in business forced the company to reduce its work force from 150,000 to 53,000. This triggered the historic "Boeing recession" that is still remembered by Washington residents. By 1971, Boeing was rebounding. A decade later, the company was the world leader in the manufacture of commercial aircraft.

By mid-1989, it had back orders for 1,526 jetliners, worth about $70 billion—at least a five-year backlog. The company has been increasing both its work space and its work force in an effort to deliver the aircraft on time. During the first quarter of 1989, Boeing employed about 107,000 in the Seattle metropolitan area. As a result, a shortage of trained workers has developed. Good machinists and engineers are scarce.

Boeing's influence goes far beyond its employment statistics, however. It is the largest exporter in the country, the largest public company in the state and the state's largest employer. Its work-

During World War II, Puget Sound Sheet Metal Works (now PSF Industries) operated two plants and employed a total of 1,400 people. Pictured: parts assembly for B-17 and B-29 bombers.

ers have formed the state's largest credit union, and have developed their own flying association and tennis club. The health of the company is important to the more than 1,000 other businesses that supply parts and reserves and to the thousands of retail outlets where Boeing employees shop.

The average annual wage for aerospace workers is approximately $40,000. One study suggests that for every dollar's worth of aviation products and services produced in the state, Washington's economic activity increases by $2.07. In 1987, aviation directly or indirectly generated almost a quarter of the jobs in the state. No wonder everyone keeps an eye on this giant company that has such an important role in the economic future of the Seattle metropolitan area—indeed the future of the entire state.

The interior of the fuselage and main assembly room at the Boeing Airplane Company on the Duwamish River in 1922.

A few months after his historic May 21, 1927 nonstop flight across the Atlantic, Charles Lindbergh landed his famous "Spirit of St. Louis" at Sand Point. His brief visit to Seattle was part of a nationwide tour to promote the building of airfields.

Left: *Boeing is a diversified company. Its Computer Services subsidiary owns one of the biggest, fastest time-sharing computer configurations in the world.*
Below: *A recent photo of Boeing 747s under construction at the Everett plant.*

Banks and Finance

The early pioneers in our state brought with them a distrust in banks. Their parents and grandparents remembered when the first U.S. Bank was founded. Eighty percent of the stock in this original federal bank was owned by wealthy citizens of the Northeast, the other 20 percent by the federal government. Bank board members openly supported political candidates, lent money to favorite congressmen and retained Senator Daniel Webster as legal counsel.

The general populace reacted heatedly to this influence-peddling. Andrew Jackson made the bank a major issue in his presidential campaign. During his two terms as president, he killed the national bank and distributed federal funds among state banks. Under little supervision, many state banks invested unwisely and printed paper money without concern for specie reserves.

In 1853, when Washington Territory was created, a provision in the enabling legislation denied the legislature the right to charter banks of any kind. The National Banking Act of the 1860s did little to remedy the situation. It allowed national banks to be founded, but required $50,000 in capitalization and forbade the use of real estate as collateral for loans. These restrictions prevented national banks from forming in the fledgling territory.

The only remaining alternative was private, unincorporated banking. Some private banks operated with dishonest motives, but most bank owners were honest businessmen, such as the founders of the Baker-Boyer bank in Walla Walla. Their bank, which opened in 1869, was the first in the territory to retain its identity for any length of time. Phillips and Horton opened Washington Territory's second bank in June 1870, in Seattle. Over the years and after many mergers, this institution became Seafirst Bank.

By 1880, one national and six private banks served Washington's 75,000 residents. In 1886, Congress allowed territories to approve banks to provide discount,

Northern Bank and Trust Company was organized in 1906 with $100,000 in capital. By 1911, this building at Fourth and Pike was known as the Northern Bank and Trust building.

Fifty years ago, this building on the southwest corner of Third and Pine was commonly called the Northwestern Mutual building, for that insurance company occupied much of the structure. Today the adjacent Fischer Studio Building is still called that but the corner structure is now known as Olympic Tower.

deposit, trust, loan and guarantee services but not to issue paper money. From that time until 1914, a considerable number of state, national and private banks were founded.

Every little town had its bank. Among these were Pacific National Bank of Tacoma, which opened its doors in 1885. Rainier Bank, recently purchased by Security Pacific, traces its roots back to a pair of banks that opened their doors in 1889—the National Bank of Commerce and Washington National Bank. Washington Mutual Savings Bank, founded as Washington National Building Loan and Investment Association, also traces its roots to 1889.

This interior photo of the Dexter Horton Bank in 1882 frames Vice President Arthur Denny in the vault doorway. To the right is young teller N.H. Latimer waiting on a customer. He would later serve as president of Seattle First National Bank, successor of Dexter Horton Bank.

Dexter Horton, Seattle's first banker, organized the second bank in the territory in 1870. Today it is known as Seafirst. Horton lived until 1904.

Dexter Horton's bank, which stood on the corner of First South and Washington, was gutted in the 1889 fire. It was repaired and used for a few years, then was replaced with this more imposing Dexter Horton Bank Building.

Peoples National Bank, now U.S. Bank of Washington, opened as Peoples Savings Bank in 1890.

The major recession that began in 1893 caused problems for all financial institutions in the new state. Over a three-year period, half the banks failed, merged or voluntarily liquidated.

State banks were loosely regulated until 1907, when the state banking department was created. That year in Tacoma, Pacific Building and Loan Association, today known as Pacific First Federal Savings Bank, was founded. Two years later, the state banned branch banking, a prohibition that remained on the books until 1933, although ways were found to circumvent it. In 1915, the state required all banks to be chartered under state or national regulations. That same year, a law was passed permitting mutual savings banks to operate in Washington.

World War I pumped millions into Washington bank accounts, doubling assets in five years. The post-war recession caused assets to drop 25 percent. Banks were just recovering when the depression of the 1930s struck. March 1, 1933 brought a nationwide panic that depleted reserves in most banks. Several states declared bank holidays on March 2, but Washington waited until March 3. It was almost too late—many banks had folded.

On March 5, President Roosevelt ordered a national banking holiday after which banks began to recover. Of the 58 state banks in distress in March 1933, 48 had reopened and 10 had been liquidated by January 1935. Federal deposit insurance became available in 1934.

In 1933, credit union legislation was signed by Governor Clarence Martin. Of the large number of credit unions operating today, the top nine each have well over $100 million in assets (Boeing Employees is the largest, with nearly $1 billion in assets).

The deregulation of the Reagan years resulted in mergers and purchases of several large regional banks. In 1983, Bank America purchased a controlling interest in the state's largest bank, Seafirst. Pacific National Bank became First Interstate of Washington in 1981. Rainier Bank was sold to Security Pacific in 1987. Peoples Bank and Old National Bank were combined in 1987 as part of Oregon's U.S. Bancorp.

With the controlling interest in the state's largest banking institutions going to out-of-state corporations, Puget Sound Bancorp, founded in 1901, became the largest independent bank in the state. Many other banks, thrifts and credit unions are thriving. Seattle's reputation as a leader in international trade has helped bring 10 foreign bank branches to the area.

Another type of financial service is supplied by brokerage firms in Seattle, such as Piper, Jaffray & Hopwood, Inc.

In 1919, John E. Price and son Andrew organized the Marine Bank and soon absorbed several banks under the Marine Bancorporation. One of its holdings was the National Bank of Commerce. Both the holding corporation and N.B. of C. took the Rainier name in 1974, which in turn merged with Security Pacific in 1986.

The stenographic pool at John E. Price and Company in 1922.

High Technology

Robert Abbott and Christine Schuch separate white blood cells from whole blood at NeoRx, one of Puget Sound's many promising new technology companies.

High technology covers a broad range of economic enterprises. It is a process or product that is state-of-the-art. In the greater Seattle area, there are more than 100 different specialties in nearly 1,000 high-tech firms. Products are sold worldwide, with Canada being the top importer of high-tech goods from this region.

Only a few high-tech companies existed in this state until after World War II. They began to proliferate in the '70s and '80s.

High tech remains one of the fastest growing industries in this state. This segment of the economy is growing at about twice the rate of all other fields. The heaviest concentration of Washington's high-tech firms is in the Puget Sound area. Seattle has the highest number, although several suburban areas have developed high-tech corridors or parks. The greater Seattle area was the seventh largest high-tech market in the country in 1988.

The Microsoft campus in Redmond.

Small firms dominate the high-tech market, but a few large, locally-owned businesses provide a substantial number of the jobs. One of the largest high-tech firms is Boeing Electronics, a division of the parent company. Others include BCS and WIS, subsidiaries of Boeing and Weyerhaeuser, respectively. The most famous high-tech firm in the Seattle area was founded by a native of the Northwest. John Fluke, in 1952, moved his fledgling company from Connecticut to Seattle and quickly established a reputation as the leading manufacturer and marketer of electronic test and measurement equipment.

Many international and national high-tech firms have entered the local market either by establishing Seattle offices or acquiring local firms. Their activities range from sales to manufacturing.

High-tech companies produce advanced medical instruments, weapons systems, water-cutting and tunnel-boring equipment, computer equipment and much more. The fast-growing software and programming segment develops custom and pre-packaged programs. Users of specialized programs include the legal, medical, accounting and financial communities, public utilities and governmental units.

Above: *Aldus software at work.*
Left: *M & R Services, a subsidiary of Milliman and Robertson, uses large mainframe computing facilities for valuation and product modeling.*

International Trade

Hullin Transfer Co., which still hauls freight today, sent a truck to Schwabacher's wharf to pick up this load of Alaskan yellow turnips in 1915.

Washington's trade with foreign countries has expanded as the state's manufacturing output has increased and transportation services have improved. Products such as commercial aircraft and high-tech equipment, in particular, have contributed to the increase in trade, and the modernization of the ports in Seattle, Tacoma and other parts in the past two decades has facilitated that increase.

Two hundred years ago, international trade attracted the first white men to the Northwest. They bartered manufactured products to the Indians for animal pelts that they carried to the Orient and traded for tea, spices, silk and other goods. These in turn were transported to American and European ports for sale, often at considerable profit.

The first permanent white settlers on Puget Sound exported pilings, lumber, coal, salted fish and dried hops. They purchased flour from South America and fresh vegetables and meats from the Hudson's Bay Company and Native Americans until they could produce their own.

Since its founding, Seattle has continually grown in importance as a seaport, as have several other of Washington's coastal cities. Before the turn of the century, Puget Sound had developed extensive foreign commerce, shipping wheat to Europe and lumber to all parts of the Pacific. Coal from Puget Sound mines warmed San

Franciscans. Trade relations with British Columbia and Alaska were continually increasing. Tea from China and Japan constituted a major import through Seattle.

In 1892, the value of the five major exports through Seattle were as follows:

Lumber	$1,133,727
Laths	8,762
Shingles	3,705
Wheat	2,916,590
Flour	503,608

(An 1892 dime had about the same purchasing power as a 1989 dollar.)

From this list, the importance of the railroads is apparent. The export of greatest value was wheat from the hinterlands. Flour exports were increasing as well.

Surprisingly, imports in 1892 via Seattle docks amounted to only $700,000. This was partly because Tacoma was the terminus of the Northern Pacific Railroad. The Great Northern rails would not terminate in Seattle until the following year. Furthermore, importers were shipping through San Francisco and Portland, which had been connected to transcontinental rails for several years. It took time for Seattle to establish a reputation as a major port.

By 1904, Seattle was more firmly established as a port and exports had picked up considerably. That year, 431 million board feet of lumber went by ship from Seattle to other domestic ports, and 180 million board feet went to foreign ports. In addition, lumber—250 million board feet— went eastward by rail from Seattle for domestic use and 408 million board feet went by rail to eastern ports for transshipment overseas. Added to the shipment lists were

The Founding of the Port of Seattle

The Port of Seattle was born out of the controversy over ownership of tidelands and the intransigence of the railroad corporations and other private owners of waterfront property.

According to Padraic Burke in his excellent book *A History of the Port of Seattle*, the writers of the state constitution in 1889 debated the tidelands issue at length. Theoretically, the federal government retained ownership until statehood. But Seattle's pioneer businessmen had taken control of property adjacent to the tidelands and projected their docks, wharves and piers out over the tideflats to deep water. Henry Yesler had built the first such wharf in 1853. In turn, these owners had dedicated a strip of the tideflat property along Elliott Bay as Railroad Avenue. The ownership situation was anything but clear. Members of the constitutional convention were split between those who favored public ownership and those who felt the tidelands should be developed by private enterprise. The resulting compromise only muddied the waters.

The constitution did indicate the delegates' intention to preserve tidelands adjacent to municipalities for public use. They established a five-member Harbor Line Commission to designate the boundaries of the tideland areas. The plan also provided for municipalities to acquire abutting tidelands.

Members of the Harbor

In the 1920s, loading and unloading freight on the Seattle waterfront required more manpower than it does today.

Line Commission served only as long as the governor who appointed them. The first commissioners appointed by the first state governor, Elisha P. Ferry, served for only about three years before their terms ended. Opponents of public ownership of tidelands, the most powerful being the railroads, developed a plan to obstruct any action until the term of the commission had ended.

Late in 1890, the Harbor Line Commission issued a report endorsing municipal development of potential port facilities. With only a few months remaining on the term of the commissioners, railroad lawyers filed a writ of prohibition before State Superior Court Judge Lichtenberg. This judge, it seems, owed his appointment in large measure to the influence of Thomas Burke, who just happened to be the railroad attorney. Lichtenberg decided in favor of an injunction preventing action. The conservative *Seattle Times* and the Seattle Chamber of Commerce both responded by supporting public ownership of tidelands on Seattle's waterfront.

The State Supreme Court unanimously reversed Judge Lichtenberg's injunction, but the railroads referred the matter to the federal court, where Judge Cornelius Hanford, who also owed Burke for supporting his appointment, ruled in favor of the railroads. Hanford's decision was subsequently overturned by the Circuit Court of Appeals. The U.S. Supreme Court refused to hear the case. The matter had been delayed so long, however, that the term of the Harbor Line Commission had expired.

The new Harbor Line Commission appointed in 1894 by Governor John H. McGraw was not so willing to support municipal ownership. It redrew the harbor lines, leaving nothing for the municipalities or a public port. This disregard for public need eventually cost taxpayers millions of dollars when the municipality bought back tidelands that by law had once belonged to the public.

After the turn of the century, support for public ownership of ports gained momentum all across the country. Seattle, for various reasons, became the site of the first autonomous municipal corporation in the country that specialized in port matters. But not before another battle was won.

The rapid population growth in the Puget Sound area created problems amid the unstable economic conditions of the 1890s. When times were good, the wealthy grew wealthier but few of the additional dollars trickled down to the working citizens. As a result, several groups were formed to improve the lot of the wage earner. Some of these were radical in their approach, such as the International Workers of the World (Wobblies). The Populist movement of the late 1890s actually saw "the People's Party" gain control of both houses of the state legislature and the governor's chair for a brief time. Later, in 1912, a majority of Washington voters cast their votes for former Republican president Theodore Roosevelt, now candidate of the

In this turn-of-the-century photo, Colman Dock on the left anchors the Seattle waterfront piers. James M. Colman built his first ramshackle wharf in 1882. Today's Colman Dock serves as the home of the Washington State ferry fleet.

Progressive "Bull Moose" party. Out of these various efforts a coalition was formed to convince the electorate of the intransigence of the railroad companies and the need for modern port facilities. In 1907, a bill was drafted in Olympia that called for improvement of tidelands and for public port facilities. It passed both houses only to be vetoed by Governor Albert Meade.

External forces began to influence the situation. The Panama Canal was scheduled to open in 1914 and most west coast cities were making extensive harbor improvements in anticipation of increased trade. Tacoma, which until that time had trailed Seattle in port development, managed to capture much of the Seattle trade. Furthermore, the Lake Washington

Ship Canal was nearly completed and soon oceangoing ships would be anchored in the salt-free waters of Lakes Union and Washington.

In 1910, King County voters approved the Duwamish River Improvement District, which would open four and a half miles of that shallow river to large oceangoing vessels.

Through it all, the advocates of private ownership did not surrender. Early in 1911, the state supreme court upheld its contention that the state constitution did not grant the legislators power to establish special improvement districts. This decision appeared to kill the move for a port district, but a backlash resulted. Even conservative businessmen began to understand the need for a modern port to serve Seattle. Private owners not only could not afford such improvements, they could not agree among themselves as to what was needed. A publicly owned and supported entity was the only answer.

The Seattle Chamber of Commerce and the Seattle Commercial Club led the way. A bill was drafted permitting counties to establish public port districts. The bill passed both houses and was signed by Governor Marion E. Hay on June 8, 1911. The formation of a port district required the approval of county voters. The boundaries of the district were to be coterminous with the county. The district had the power of eminent domain, it could issue bonds approved by 60 percent of the voters and could levy property taxes. It

could build, maintain and operate all systems of sea walls, wharves, docks, ferries, canals, locks and tidal basins.

On September 5, 1911, the voters of King County elected the first port commissioners— H.M. Chittenden, C.E. Remsberg and Robert Bridges. Port improvements were immediately undertaken. At Smith Cove, the largest pier on the Pacific Coast was built; the east waterway was dredged, a public dock was constructed on the central waterfront and a four-story warehouse was converted to house the Port Commission.

Long-range plans were developed for the Duwamish River and the entire waterfront. New terminals were added, including the Hanford Street grain terminal.

Over the years, the Port has secured much more waterfront property. In 1947, the Port dedicated the Seattle-Tacoma International Airport. In the 1960s, it moved into containerization when it was but an infant industry. From the mid-1960s to the mid-1980s, the Port's container traffic increased at an average annual compound growth rate of 15 percent. In 1965, it began warehousing import cargoes for customers. Today, it operates 1.5 million square feet of warehouse space. In 1966, it began acting as a shipper's agent, consolidating truck and later rail cargoes for import customers. By 1988, the Port of Seattle was the fourth largest container port in the United States and the 18th largest in the world.

5.7 billion shingles and 199 million laths.

Disputes over tidelands and lack of coordinated planning resulted in chaotic private development on the Seattle waterfront. This convinced the voters of King County that a publicly owned port was needed. In 1911, they agreed to create the Port of Seattle, which would operate under an elected Board of Commissioners.

Ten years later, in 1924, Seattle ranked second in the nation in the value of imports and eighth in value of exports. By then, the silk trains were speeding eastward carrying the raw product from which hosiery and fine garments were made. As the list below shows, Seattle was the major U.S. port for receiving silk.

Ships from all over the world came to Elliott Bay at the turn of the century to load up with lumber, coal, grain, hops and other products of the Northwest. In the background can be seen the Denny (also called the Washington) Hotel atop Denny Hill.

Principal Imports of Washington District in 1924
(mostly through Seattle)

Raw silk	$207 million
Copper ore	26 million
Chinese wood oil	16 million
China dishes	6 million
Newsprint	2 million
Tea	2 million
All else*	2 million
Total	$255 million

Condensed milk to Japan, canned salmon to Great Britain, fresh and dried fruits to Canada and Great Britain, and automobiles to Pacific Rim countries.

In the 65 years since that report of 1924, the world of trade has advanced tremendously. Washington has become a major trading state. While the national trade deficit is counted in the billions of dollars each month, Washington counters this by exporting state products of much greater value than the imports consumed by state residents. In 1988, Washington exported more than $3,000 worth of state products per capita, the highest per capita figure of any state.

Washington-produced exports increased 31 percent in 1988 to a record $14 billion. The value of imports consumed by Washingtonians was about $6.5 billion. This resulted in a state trade surplus of more than $7 billion.

In 1988, top exports through Washington State ports were:

Until after the turn of the century, sailing ships were used for long journeys. Steamships stayed close to shore, where wood and coal were available for refueling. Later, when steam engines were improved and oil came into use, steamships quickly took over for many reasons, among them their greater maneuverability in confined Puget Sound waters.

Commodity	Value ($ in millions)
Airplanes	$7,035.4
Saw and veneer logs	1,373.0
Corn and maize	1,148.8
Aluminum	675.0
Fish (fresh, chilled and frozen)	514.0
All other commodities	11,600.2
Total	$22,350.2

In 1988, the most valuable imports through Washington ports were:

Commodity	Value ($ in millions)
Passenger motor vehicles	$1,489.0
Motor vehicle parts	1,454.6
Toys, games, Xmas ornaments	1,452.6
Footwear	1,200.1
Audio and video equipment	887.4
All other commodities	26,107.9
Total	$32,591.6

Which countries purchase Washington-produced commodities? The Port of Seattle has a list of 107. The top 10 and the value of exports going to them in 1988 (in millions of dollars) are as follows:

Top Buyers of Washington Commodities	
Japan	$6,393.4
Canada	3,903.1
South Korea	1,787.1
United Kingdom	1,567.2
Taiwan	1,229.3
Australia	866.4
West Germany	747.3
China	705.6
Hong Kong (British)	667.6
Brazil	556.4

The top 10 countries whose products are imported into Washington are listed at the top of the next column (with the values in millions of dollars).

Two companies with headquarters in the Seattle metropolitan area, Boeing and Weyerhaeuser, were listed among the nation's top 50 exporters in 1986. Washington exported more com-

Top Exporters to Washington	
Japan	$15,358.9
Canada	3,683.0
South Korea	3,507.6
Taiwan	3,143.5
Hong Kong (British)	1,364.4
China	1,152.2
Singapore	675.5
Australia	515.4
France	502.5
Indonesia	314.3

mercial aircraft and forest products than any other state and was second in the export of salmon and vegetables. Other exports in the top 10 included wheat, fruit, cattle, hides, fish, vehicles and aircraft parts.

The Port of Seattle is currently the 18th largest container port in the world and the fourth largest in the country. The chart below lists statistics for the Port of Seattle in 1988 ($ in millions):

Exports*	Amount	Imports	Amount
Softwood lumber	$619	Office machines, data process. equip., parts	$1,819
Mfg. paper	388	Apparel	1,805
Hides	359	Motor vehicle parts	1,193
Plastic resin	356	Home audio equip.	1,166
Aluminum	334	Elec./electronic equip., parts	1,158
Wood pulp	330	Toys, Xmas decorations	977
Fish (frozen)	319	Telephone comm., equip.	973
Grain, cereals	189	Footwear	828
Industrial equip.	150	Mfg. articles	583
Beef, pork and poultry	150	Motor veh. engines/parts	516

These figures are for waterborne cargo only.

The Seattle waterfront has seen some hot fires. On July 30, 1914, the Grand Trunk Railway terminal burned. This was a Canadian railway that used ships to transport freight and passengers between Seattle and Vancouver.

Manufacturing and Processing

According to Clarence Bagley's *History of King County*, the first manufacturing enterprise in the county was Henry Yesler's sawmill. The second was Dr. David Maynard's ill-starred salmon salting effort, which failed to preserve the fish long enough to reach San Francisco. However, the effort promoted cooperage, for he salted them in barrels, and this in turn provided work for blacksmiths, who made the hoops. M.D. Woodin started a tannery in 1856 and H. Jones opened a boot and shoe shop in 1867. Flour was first milled in 1864 in a tiny mill assembled by Henry Yesler.

In 1872, Marshall Blum erected an ice house on Yesler's wharf and shipped in ice all the way from the Sierra Mountains of California. It was stored in sawdust. Once ice making technology

In 1919, during strawberry season, the Spokane Street Terminal was a busy place. Dozens of women were hired to wash the berries and place them in barrels for cold storage.

Julius W. Augustine and Henry A. Kyer were executives in a large wholesale and retail grocery business. Back in 1915, Augustine and Kyer's hand-dipped chocolates were just one of their many popular products.

was developed in the early 1880s, ice houses became popular in Seattle. The first ice cream was made in Seattle in 1872 using Blum's ice.

Seattle's first baker started his business in 1864, a candy maker opened shop in 1876, and a soap maker in 1870. (Many pioneer women continued to make their own soap of fat, lye and ashes).

Hugh McAleer was the first tanner and Henry Van Asselt the first furniture maker. Soon there were brick yards, wagon makers, foundries and iron works. A broom factory opened, a woolen mill began weaving in 1892 and a cordage company was founded. Shipbuilding was undertaken soon after the arrival of the first settlers.

The 1860 census, the first census taken after Washington became a territory, listed the principal manufactured products of the region as lumber (more than 80 percent of the total), flour, leather and canned fish. The census of a decade later added clothing, boots and shoes, and the processing of butter and cheese. Clothing was

the most valuable item manufactured in the territory. Loggers and sawmill workers were the major customers.

The 1880 census added shipbuilding, blacksmithing, saddlery and harness making as leading industries. Shipbuilders used local

lumber to construct craft for local fishermen and for intrastate shipping companies. Among several long-lived maritime companies formed before 1900 were Foss Tug and Puget Sound Bridge and Dredge.

By 1890, the first year of statehood, many of these new industries had made considerable progress. During the preceding decade, the following had gained admission to the "important product" list: clay products (the Denny Clay Co., founded in 1889, now part of Interpace); foundry and metal work (Washington Iron Works, which was founded in 1881 and just recently closed its doors); beer (Rainier Brewery was founded in 1878 and Olympia Brewery in 1896); finished wood products; and printed materials.

The state report prepared for the 1893 Columbian Exposition in Chicago listed these King County industries: sawmills, shingle mills, sash and door factories, breweries, furniture factories, iron works,

The manager of the Bayview Brewery inspects a bottle of his product in the 1880s.

brick yards, electric light and gas works, car shops, boiler works, cracker factories, soap factories, ice houses, confectioneries and tile makers. There were also canneries, meat packers, box manufacturers, woodworking shops, ship and boat builders, flour mills, bottling works, cigar factories, brass foundries and cornice factories. More than 60 miles of electric and cable car lines, then privately owned, were transporting local residents. "Newspapers [including the *Post-Intelligencer* and the *Press Times*, now *The Seattle Times*] and magazines of every denomination, nationality and degree in daily, weekly and monthly issues . . ." were found on newsstands. In all, the report said, King County was home to 226 manufacturing concerns with a total output value of $7.7 million.

With the population increasing beyond all expectations, manufacturing output trebled between 1900 and 1910. Values of dairy, clay, metal, bakery and brewery output increased 600 percent or more. The diversification of industry caused lumber output, which was actually increasing, to drop to a 40 percent share of the total value of manufactured goods in 1920; half a century earlier, it had been 80 percent.

The 1905 *Washington State Yearbook* reported that King County was the state's leading lumber producer, with 189 firms paying 7,687 employees $4.6 million in wages. Following King County as lumber producers were Snohomish, Chehalis (now Grays Harbor), Whatcom, Pierce, Skagit, Lewis and Spokane counties. Because the railroads had been serving the area for a decade, Seattle had developed as the transshipment port for grain, flour and hay from inland counties.

By 1910, the value of Washington State products ranked 21st among the states. A decade earlier it had ranked only 30th.

In the next seven decades, during which transportation and communication services were

John M. Frink founded Washington Iron Works in 1881. After the original plant burned in 1889, the structure seen here was built near the foot of Beacon Hill at Ninth and Norman. In the 1920s, the company moved to a modern plant at Sixth and Atlantic. Washington Iron Works remained there until it went out of business a few years back.

Blacksmithing was still a big business in 1906, as this photo of Seattle's Hoffman Blacksmith Shop attests.

The Port of Seattle was building these grain elevators on the east waterway in 1915.

The fine clays found in the Puget Sound country were the basis for the many brick yards that developed during the 1880s. This large yard in the Marginal Way area helped provide the brick to rebuild Seattle after the 1889 fire.

transformed, Washington became a major producer of new products, most notably commercial aircraft.

Although services continue to account for an increasing proportion of employment in the state and region, manufacturing still employs nearly 20 percent of the work force. The following is a list of the top 10 Seattle area manufacturers in 1988, ranked by number of employees.

These top 10 manufacturers were followed by Todd Shipyards,

Company	Employees	Products
The Boeing Company	107,000	Aircraft, space systems, computer and info systems
Burlington Northern Inc.	3,500	Forest products, natural resources, railroad ops.
Weyerhaeuser Co.	3,200	Diversified forest products, real estate
PACCAR, Inc.	3,000	Heavy-duty trucks and parts, mining and oil field equipment, leasing
Westmark International	2,400	Advanced medical technologies
John Fluke Mfg. Co.	1,900	Electronic test and measurement equipment
Microsoft Corp.	1,800	Microcomputer software
Bayliner Marine Corp.	1,550	Fiberglass pleasure boats
Eldec Corp.	1,500	Electronic products for aerospace use
Sundstrand Data Control	1,500	Avionic systems

Scott Paper Co., Heath Techna Aerospace Co., Honeywell Marine Systems, Physio Control Corp., Criton Technologies, Hewlett Packard Co., Nalley's Fine Foods, Olin Defense Systems and Gai's Seattle French Baking Company.

The *Washington State Yearbook* reported the following employment figures for the state's major industries in 1986:

Industry	Employees
1. Transportation equipment (Aerospace accounted for 85,000)	97,700
2. Lumber and wood products	37,900
3. Food and kindred products	30,500
4. Machinery (Electrical equipment accounted for 12,300)	30,100
5. Printing and publishing	18,700
6. Paper and allied products	16,900
7. Primary metals (Aluminum accounted for 7,600)	11,800
8. Chemicals and allied products	11,500
9. Instruments and related products	10,400
10. Fabricated metals	10,000
11. Miscellaneous non-durable goods	8,000
12. Stone, clay and glass	6,300
13. Apparel and allied products	6,100
14. Miscellaneous durable goods	4,600
15. Furniture and fixtures	3,900

The late Eddie Bauer, founder of the sporting goods chain, is shown here in one of the down vests he manufactured for sale in his store.

A cab being set on the chassis at Kenworth Truck Company, a division of PACCAR, Inc.

Real Estate

Since the days when the pioneers erected simple homes of logs or boards, the standard of living in Washington has continually increased. The first apartments in Seattle were tiny and plain. The hotels offered closet-sized rooms with a bathtub at the end of the hall and other amenities out back. A century ago, a simple home could be rented for five dollars a month and hotel rooms cost 25 cents a night—50 cents with board.

Single-family dwellings have escalated in value, particularly in recent years. Using 1967 as the base year, houses in King County have increased in value as follows:

Low price group:
Average cost in 1967—$13,000
Average cost now—$71,000

Medium price group:
Average cost in 1967—$24,000
Average cost now—$108,000

High price group:
Average cost in 1967—$56,000
Average cost now—$244,000

The state passed legislation in 1963 to allow the sale of condominium units. More than 14,500 King County apartments were sold as condos between 1963 and 1982. Today, most condos on the market are of recent construction. The cost per unit varies from $40,000 to more than $200,000. About two-thirds of the condominiums sold in 1987 and 1988 brought $80,000 or more.

Apartment rents have been rising and are expected to increase further because of a strong market. Apartment rentals are especially strong on the east side of Lake Washington and in Bothell.

Purchase costs of apartment buildings are likewise increasing, and institutional investors have

After the great Seattle fire destroyed the Occidental Hotel on the triangular block between Yesler, James, First and Second, owner John Collins cleared the debris, as we see in the photo, then built what later became the Seattle Hotel. This in turn was demolished in 1960 to make room for a parking lot.

become interested in large apartment buildings because of predicted population increases in the Seattle area.

The office space market is also strong. A recent inventory of 296 competitive office buildings in downtown Seattle of at least 10,000 square feet found a vacancy rate of about 12.5 percent. On the Eastside (Bellevue, Redmond, Kirkland, the I-90 and SR-520 corridors, Mercer Island and Overlake), the 219 competitive office buildings with at least 10,000 square feet had a vacancy rate close to 21 percent. Twenty-four projects under construction or being proposed will add three million more square feet of Eastside office space.

The lodging market in the Seattle metropolitan area has improved considerably since the Washington State Convention and Trade Center opened in 1988. Downtown hotels experienced a 70.2 percent occupancy rate during 1988, the first time in the 1980s that the figure exceeded 70

Some of Seattle's finest homes were built on the slopes of Queen Anne Hill in the 1880s. Typical of the architecture is the home of realtor George Kinnear. Bayview Manor has since been built on the site. In 1884, Kinnear gave the city a 14-acre park on the south slope of Queen Anne hill.

Suburban property values began to increase as roads were improved and the automobile became popular. The year is 1918 and the auto has just crossed the Woodinville Bridge that spans the Sammamish River. This section of gravel road was part of the Bothell Highway.

In 1928, the Alderwood Manor area had a new paved highway but still much vacant land.

The Green Lake area did not attract homeowners until the late 1880s, after realtor W.D. Wood and engineer Dr. E.C. Kilbourne platted a town and created a 10-acre amusement park. At the south end of the lake, Guy Phinney was developing an estate he called Woodland Park. This was later purchased by the city as a site for the zoo. This view is of the northeast end of the lake in 1900.

Jackson Realty and Loan was a typical realty office in the early 1900s. The picture is dated 1910.

Once the city built streets to Laurelhurst and developers had subdivided the properties, homes appeared as if by magic. Here are three new homes built in 1926.

Building the Smith Tower

L.C. Smith built his famous tower in Seattle because his wife's dressmaker had retired here. It seems that Miss Mary Slocum, when she lived in Syracuse, New York, made dresses for Mrs. Smith. She decided to enjoy her later years in Seattle with her sister Mrs. W.E. Boone.

In 1888, Mrs. Smith and her son traveled across the continent by rail to San Francisco and decided to wander up the coast to Seattle to see the sights and visit with Mrs. Slocum. They greatly enjoyed the Puget Sound country and, once home, described the opportunities to L.C. himself.

Now James W. Clise enters the picture. He arrived in Seattle the day after the great Seattle fire of June 6, 1889. Recognizing the need for funds to rebuild the heart of the city, he organized the Clise Investment Co., proceeding to raise hundreds of thousands of dollars from several eastern investors.

In 1890, Clise visited New York in an effort to raise more money for rebuilding. Before leaving Seattle, Clise had conversations with former Governor Watson Squire, at the time one of the two first state senators. Squire, who was land poor and needed liquidity to rebuild his downtown structures, asked Clise to act as an agent in selling off some of his holdings. Clise stopped in Syracuse to visit an attorney friend named William Nottingham. Nottingham suggested they call on a neighbor, L.C. Smith, who had

The steel ribs of the Smith Tower were in place when this picture was snapped in 1913.

amassed a fortune from the sale of typewriters that bore his name.

The men held numerous meetings, and Smith ended up purchasing eight commercial properties in Seattle from Squire. Smith paid with a single check; at that time, it was the most valuable real estate transaction in Seattle history.

In 1909, Smith visited Seattle. Clise, who was now his local representative, suggested that the property at Second and Yesler, site of a one-story structure, was valuable enough to be upgraded. Smith's son Burns had been looking closely at new skyscrapers rising in New York City. When his father returned home late in 1909, Burns already had a plan in mind for a Seattle structure—a 21-story building with a tower of equal height. Mrs.

Smith backed the plan. Soon after, L.C. Smith engaged the Syracuse architects Gaggan and Gaggan to draw up the plans.

Construction of the Smith Tower began on November 1, 1911, and was completed in 1914. L.C. Smith died shortly before it was finished but his son carried on with the job. A promotional pamphlet printed in 1912 indicated it would be the tallest structure in the world outside of New York. The first two floors were to be finished in granite and the exterior above was to be of terra cotta with ornamentation. The 600 offices were to be served by eight high-speed elevators. The total cost of the building: $1.5 million.

For nearly half a century, the unique shape and height of the Smith Tower made it not only a major Seattle landmark but the tallest building in town.

Banker Joshua Green built the 11-story Green Building on the corner of Fourth and Pike in 1912. At the time, it was one of the largest office structures in that part of town.

percent. The average price of a downtown hotel room rose eight percent during the year to about $75. Several new hotels have been proposed for the downtown core, including an all-suite luxury hotel.

Hotel occupancy in South Seattle and the airport area dipped slightly to 70.5 percent in 1988, as growth in rooms outpaced demand. Several new properties entered the market after mid-1987, including the Comfort, La Quinta, Cypress, Hampton and Ramada, which together added more than 700 rooms.

Eastside hotels ended the year with an occupancy rate of 71.9 percent. The 382-room Hyatt Regency in downtown Bellevue and a 147-room hotel in Tukwila opened during the year.

Lodging demand in North Seattle and Everett grew by 10 percent, boosting occupancy to about 60 percent. The Lynnwood Resi-dence Inn and the Cypress Inn recently opened, and at least one other property is slated for development near I-5.

The surging population and the rapidly rising property costs in the Seattle area have resulted in some very successful years for real estate firms such as John L. Scott.

Resource Industries

Seattle's Stetson-Post lumber mill at Hanford and Whatcom was still receiving logs from old growth forests in 1920.

The first Europeans came to the Northwest to trade for the furs of native animals. The Hudson's Bay Company's traders and trappers were the first to take up permanent residence in the area. In the 1830s, they branched out into agriculture at Fort Nisqually, the first white settlement on Puget Sound. Domesticated animals were raised, and grains, fruits and vegetables harvested. The rich land produced more than could be consumed locally, and rather than discard the surplus, the company sought potential consumers. They found them in Russian Alaska and at home in England.

Soon after, the Hudson's Bay Company built simple water-powered sawmills and flour mills. These produced a surplus of lumber and flour, which was traded in Hawaii and other Pacific Rim countries.

When the Oregon Country was divided at the 49th parallel in 1846, Puget Sound became part of the United States. The first American settlers continued the businesses started by the British; they exported pilings, lumber, grains and other produce. Coal was soon added to these exports. Intermittent rumors about precious metals attracted many new settlers to the region, but none led to major discoveries.

The new state of Washington

proudly described its natural resources in a promotional book written for the 1893 Columbian Exposition in Chicago. At the time, the state claimed a population of 395,000, and was growing rapidly thanks to the recently arrived railroad service.

Timber, the book reported, grew in all but two Washington counties. Nearly 410 trillion board feet stood on more than 23 million acres. More than one-third of the population depended on the timber industry for a living.

In 1891, Washington mined more than 1 million short tons (a short ton equals 2,000 pounds) of coal, more than half from mines in King and Pierce counties. The report listed coal mining as the leading industry in King County.

Many other minerals were listed as "found in merchantable quantities." Sandstone, other building stones, clay and limestone became important products.

The 1892 report describes 10 fish canneries on the Washington side of the Columbia River. Fish traps, fish wheels and seines were legally capturing most of the fish spawning up the river. Washington fish canneries produced 465,000 48-can cases that year.

In addition, the Columbia River yielded 2,000 tons of sturgeon, much of it sent to eastern markets in railroad cars refrigerated with block ice. Sturgeon roe, 714 kegs in all (each keg weighing 135 pounds), was shipped east to make caviar.

The Puget Sound area produced 6.6 million pounds of salmon, 800,000 pounds of hali-

Until chainsaws came into use, experienced axmen could quickly and smoothly incise the undercut that directed the fall of the tree.

Yesler's steam sawmill belched smoke into the sky at the foot of Yesler Way in 1879.

A donkey engine provided power for cables that dragged and lifted logs to the railway. This engine was used by the Polson Logging Company of Hoquiam.

Western Washington logs were being shipped to foreign markets before World War I. Loading required much muscle power and perspiration.

A 1920s view of Fishermen's Wharf near the Ballard Bridge.

Original salmon runs were huge. This photo shows the emptying of a fish trap. Such devices soon depleted the numbers of spawning salmon and the government was forced to regulate the catches. Eventually, most fish trapping devices were outlawed.

Women at work in a Puget Sound salmon cannery around 1910.

many Eastern Washington counties, which the 1893 report described as some of the finest fruit growing country in the world. Western Washington, the report stated, was fine for growing apples, peas, plums, prunes, cherries and small fruits such as strawberries, raspberries and cranberries, but not for grapes or peaches.

Today, jobs in agriculture, forestry, fishing and mining account for less than 1 percent of the King County work force. The forests have been largely harvested and much agricultural land has been developed. Furthermore, mechanization, automation and the export of raw materials has reduced the need for labor. The squeeze on public timber has resulted in the closure of many mills, both large

but and half a million pounds of smelt that year, plus cod, perch, flounder, herring and other fish. The district also produced 560 sacks of oysters and about 200 sacks of clams each week; the latter was supplied by Native Americans, who were paid $1 per sack.

The major agricultural crop in the Puget Sound area in 1893 was hops, which could be transported great distances when dried.

Irrigation was already used in

Once Seattle had its railroad, Eastern Washington grains began to flow through the Port of Seattle. This 1909 Pemco-Webster-Stevens photo shows a 24-mule team pulling a harvester.

By 1918, Lake Chelan apples were proudly displayed in Seattle and at county fairs across the state.

and small. Logs from federal lands cannot be exported, but logs from Weyerhaeuser, the largest private exporter of logs, were the second most valuable state export (behind aircraft) in 1986, bringing in $772.4 million.

Weyerhaeuser began operations in Washington in 1900. Today, it is the second largest public company in the state. Its real estate arm, the Quadrant Corporation, is one of the larger companies in its category. Weyerhaeuser reported revenues of nearly $7 billion in 1987; it employs about 40,000 workers.

Agriculture is increasingly important to the state economy. Of the 50 states, Washington ranks No. 1 in production of hops (about 75 percent of all hops used in the country), spearmint oil (57 percent), apples (36 percent), sweet cherries (50 percent) and carrots (21 percent). It ranks second in production of peppermint oil, fall potatoes, pears, apricots and asparagus. It also ranks high with a dozen other crops, an indication of the diversity of our agricultural output.

Field crops, headed by wheat and potatoes, were valued at more than a billion dollars in 1986. Livestock and related products were worth nearly $900 million. Fruits, nuts and berries brought in $705 million (more than half of this from apples). Vegetables were valued at $162 million, with asparagus, sweet corn, onions, green peas and carrots accounting for well over half the total.

Washington's food processors are experiencing one of the best periods on record. By June 1989, they already had orders exceeding the 1988 total.

Most of the area's food fish production moves through Seattle. Amounts have varied over the past few years, with salmon accounting for about half of the value. In 1985, Washington's fish products were worth $108 million.

Mine production in 1986 was valued at $377.5 million, with sand, stone and gravel, coal and cement accounting for most of the total.

Hops were a major crop in the Puget Sound country in the 1880s. Native Americans were hired to do much of the picking.

Retail Sales

In November 1851, the very month Charles C. Terry and the other founders of Seattle arrived at Alki in what is now West Seattle, the enterprising New Yorker opened a general merchandise store in his log cabin. The store may not have been much to brag about, but it served an important function in the lives of the first Seattleites.

Over the years, retail sales increased, as did the population, income and availability of goods.

Retail sales in the Seattle metropolitan area in 1988 were estimated at $10 billion. These figures are expected to increase. Seattle is also the second most desirable area in which to locate a business. Several new stores opened in King County in 1988, including branches of Fred Meyer, the Home Club, Lamonts, Mervyn's, REI, Toys R Us and Target.

The shopping centers that ring the city are doing well. These include new theme centers such as the Pavilion Outlet Center, which features discount outlets, and Parkway Plaza, site of the Northwest's largest collection of furniture and home furnishing stores.

The following list of major regional shopping centers in the metropolitan area is an indication of how mall retailing blossomed between the time Northgate opened as Seattle's first shopping center in the 1950s and the open-

Until the 1920s, when self-service chain stores developed, groceries (often general stores) tended to be small, family-operated businesses. Here is the Beehive store in Georgetown in 1904.

For six decades prior to the First World War, Native American women sold baskets on Seattle's streets. Many pioneer families still preserve large collections of these artifacts.

There has been a Malmo Nursery in Seattle since Mr. and Mrs. Charles Malmo founded the business at the turn of the century. In the 1950s, their son sold to M.L. Bean, who added it to his Ernst Home Centers.

Early each morning at the turn of the century, representatives of the grocery stores would drive their wagons to commission row to stock up on fresh produce. In 1905, the large Ryan and Newton Commission House occupied the light-colored building at 823 Western Avenue.

Seattle's First Retailer

When the little schooner *Exact* dropped anchor off Alki in 1851 and the Denny party rowed ashore, among them was a young New Yorker named Charles C. Terry. Terry had sailed around Cape Horn to California in 1849, one of the first from his state to arrive after gold was discovered at Sutter's Mill. His luck was poor, so he worked his way north to Portland, and there met the Dennys, who had arrived shortly before after crossing the plains in a wagon train.

Before boarding the *Exact* in Portland, Terry had purchased a small supply of mercantile goods, which he hoped to sell in the new country. From his memorandum book, now preserved at the University of Washington library, we know that he brought ashore one box of tinware, one box of axes, one box of tobacco, one keg of brandy, one keg of whiskey and one box of raisins. As soon as his cabin was up, he hung out his mercantile sign.

His first customer walked in the door that same day. His name was Luther Collins and he had settled his family out on the Duwamish River a few weeks before the Denny Party arrived. Collins bought six pans, one large and two small tin pails, six pint basins, a coffee pot, two frying pans, two candlesticks and one dipper. It appears that Collins paid for these goods with 12 salmon.

Terry's account book indicates that prices were high in the isolated Puget Sound country. A bottle of ink sold for a dollar, a coffee mill for $2.50.

In April, the sailing ship *Leonesa* arrived with supplies for Terry, including flour, ammunition, calico, a barrel of molasses and a barrel of "Sandwich Island" sugar. This was fortunate, for much of Terry's trade was with the local Indians, who loved molasses and sugar. For this they bartered fish, game, wild goose and duck feathers (for feather beds).

In October 1852, Terry bought an advertisement in the *Columbian*, Washington's first newspaper, which was published in Olympia:

"Charles C. Terry, thankful for past favors, takes this opportunity to inform their numerous friends and customers that they still continue at their well-known stand in the Town of New York on Puget Sound where they keep constantly on hand and for sale at the lowest prices all kinds of merchandise usually required in a new country. N.B. Vessels furnished with cargoes of piles, square timber, shingles etc."

"New York" was Terry's name for the settlement at Alki; in fact it was named "New York-Alki," meaning "New York after a while." Terry held out for a few years after the rest of the party moved across the bay to what became Seattle, then traded his West Seattle holdings to Dr. David Maynard for property in the heart of present Seattle.

In 1856, Terry married Mary Jane Russell, daughter of a homesteader in the White River Valley. They built Seattle's first nice home at Third and James.

Terry was a good businessman. He owned the first cracker mill in Seattle, operated the tiny steamboat *Water Lily* and was one of the founders of the first Puget Sound Steam Navigation Company. His one weakness was his love of land. He purchased part of Carson Boren's land claim, now in the heart of Seattle. He picked up a quarter section from Francis McNatt and later bought 50 acres on the Duwamish, where he lived and farmed for a time.

He also was a generous man. He and Henry Yesler gave a downtown lot to the widowed Mrs. George McConaha and he was one of the founding contributors of Trinity Church. He and a partner donated one and an half acres to the original University of Washington campus.

When Seattle became a town in 1865, Charles Terry was elected a councilman and served as president of that group. He was elected to the territorial legislature in 1854.

Terry apparently suffered from tuberculosis, and his condition worsened during the winter of 1866. He died in February 1867, on the same day that his wife gave birth to their fifth child. He was 37 years old.

ing of Alderwood Mall in Lynnwood, the newest, in 1979. The most profitable of these centers is Bellevue Square. Its first unprepossessing one-story buildings opened in 1946. It has since been rebuilt and enlarged, and now ranks among the top 10 shopping centers nationwide in terms of sales and traffic.

The shopping centers listed at right are in order of square footage of developed area.

New malls are being planned in Redmond, Bothell and Renton. Crossroads is renovating and adding 140,000 square feet. Southcenter is also adding square footage, and the Overlake district is developing a new strip center.

Seattle's downtown shopping core, unlike most other large urban downtown retail centers, is thriving. Between 400,000 and 500,000 adults shop there at least once a month. The new Westlake Center in the heart of downtown is flanked by the flagship stores of Nordstrom, Frederick and Nelson and The Bon Marche. I. Magnin was recently remodeled. Pacific First Centre will soon be

Shopping Center	No. of Stores	Sq. Footage
Southcenter	127	1,400,000
Northgate	122	1,100,000
Alderwood Mall	145	1,095,000
Bellevue Square	200	1,000,000
Sea-Tac Mall	115	812,000
Parkway Plaza	45	790,000
Everett Mall	111	650,000
Aurora Village	80	511,000
Crossroads Mall	90	347,000
University Village	68	320,000
Renton Shopping Center	60	309,000
Factoria Square	63	250,000
Totem Lake Mall	65	275,000
Westwood Village	42	231,000
Pavilion Outlet Center	46	185,000
Westlake Center	100	125,000

devoting 50,000 square feet to retail and Two Union Square will devote approximately 45,000 square feet.

Several of the nation's leading retailers make the Seattle area their corporate home. Nordstrom, founded in Seattle in 1901, is the largest specialty retailer in the United States, with 48 stores in seven states. Over the past few years, Nordstrom has expanded along the West Coast and has opened its first East Coast stores in Virginia. Recreational Equipment Inc. (REI) opened its original outdoor recreational equipment and clothing store in Seattle in 1938. It now has 19 stores around the country and also features catalog sales. The late Eddie Bauer founded his sports equipment store

As Seattle grew, so did its stores. The Bon Marche built its present downtown store in 1928 on this block, which had just been cleared of older, smaller structures.

in Seattle in 1921. He soon added leisure apparel for men and women and catalog sales. In 1971, General Mills purchased the business, then sold it to the Spiegel Corporation in 1988. There are 62 Eddie Bauer stores in 14 states (30 more will be opening soon). The corporate headquarters is in Redmond. Other large retail chains with stores in the area include Jay Jacobs, with 165 stores in 11 western states. This specialist in young people's fashions opened 16 new stores in 1988. Lamonts, once part of the Pay'n Save conglomerate but now independently owned, has increased its number of family apparel outlets to 46.

In 1934, 11 independent grocers founded Associated Grocers in an effort to be competitive during the Depression years.

Today, the Seattle area's leading grocery retailers are broadening their array of gourmet and health foods and many stores now offer delicatessens, salad bars, seafood and in-store bakeries. On the other hand, some of the most successful grocery stores, such as Costco, use the wholesale market approach.

The leading grocery chains in metropolitan Seattle and the number of their stores are shown at right, along with a list of the top drug store chains in the Seattle area and the number of their outlets.

By far the leading convenience store chain in the Seattle area is 7-Eleven, with 194 outlets. Plaid Pantry has 21 and Circle-K Corp. has 20.

Grocery Chain	Outlets
Safeway	83
Albertson's	37
Thriftway	28
QFC	22
Olson's	10
Fred Meyer	7
Johnny's Foodcenters	7
Prairie Market	5
Costco Wholesale Corp.	4
Haggen's	2
Top Foods	2

Drug Store Chain	Outlets
Pay'n Save	43
Bartell Drug	31
PayLess	21
Fred Meyer	16
Thrifty Drug	9
Drug Emporium	7

Theater buildings usually reserved street level space for retail outlets. The Orpheum Theater, here being completed in 1927, would, according to the sign, house a Bartell Drug Store. This theater was demolished in 1967 to make room for the Westin Hotel.

When radio was new, show windows such as this one at the Liberty Music Shop in 1925 were shopper stoppers. Fada was the brand of all the radios in the display.

Henry Van Asselt, the Dutch immigrant who became a Duwamish River farmer in 1851, later made furniture to order and retailed it to the pioneers. Several of his pieces are preserved in museums today.

Just after the turn of the century, families visited the Garvey and Buchanan Store, which celebrated Christmas by placing Santa, Prancer, Dancer and Eskimo attendant Kozuktuk in their show window.

Services

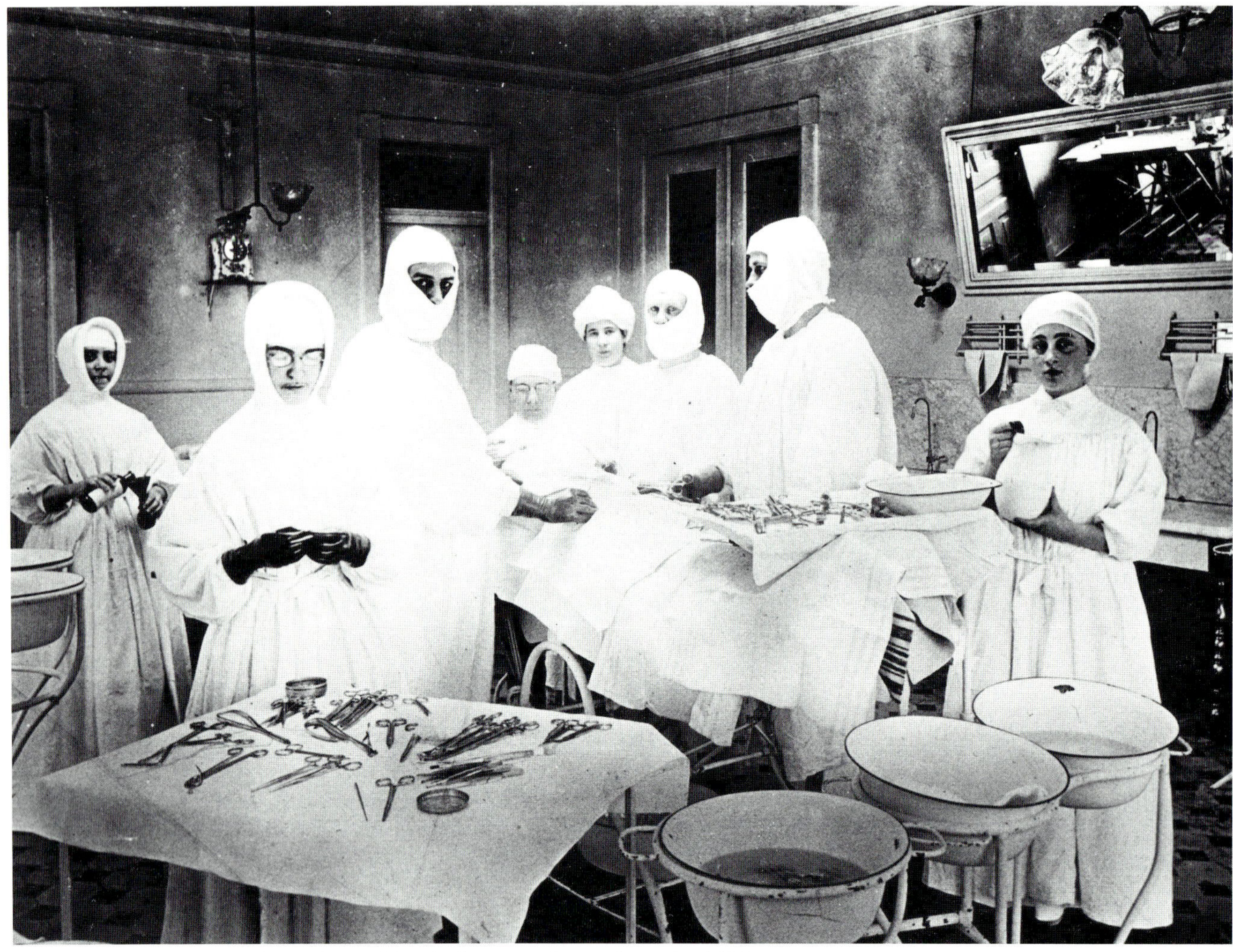

The operating room at Providence Hospital was a busy place in 1900.

Employment in the service sector continues to grow. In King County, almost one-fourth of the present work force is employed by businesses that provide a service, including medicine and legal services but excluding government, education, finance, transportation and utilities. Add these, and more than half of all jobs in the county are in the service industries.

Such was not the case with the pioneer settlers, who were largely self-sufficient. They used a doctor or dentist only as a last resort, dreading the questionable results common in those days. Lawyers were considered necessary, but not always as protectors and legal specialists. They made good legislators and helped write the laws.

Dr. David S. Maynard, King County's first doctor, was known as a kindly soul who hated to cause pain. He relied heavily on natural remedies, although he also set many a bone, stitched many a laceration and bled many a vein.

Maynard left Illinois for Seattle in 1852, chose a 640-acre donation claim south of Yesler Way, built a log cabin at First and Main, where he opened a small general merchandise emporium, served as the first justice of the peace, helped secure separation of Washington Territory from Oregon, had the county seat located on his property and was named the first notary public. He helped plat Seattle in 1853 and suggested it be named for the old Indian chief, served as county school superintendent and as sub-Indian agent, established Seattle's first hospital and continued to practice medicine until his death in 1873.

Shortly after Maynard arrived, Dr. Henry A. Smith appeared in Seattle and selected a land claim at Smith Cove north of Seattle. There was only sufficient practice for one doctor in the tiny community on Elliott Bay, so he turned to other pursuits to increase his income. He planted the first orchard of grafted trees in the territory. He opened an infirmary in his home. He invested heavily in real estate, enlarging his Smith Cove holdings to more than 1,000 acres. He also secured 600 acres of tideflat at the mouth of the Snohomish River and reclaimed much of it as Smith Island. He built the London Hotel at the foot of Pike Street and the Smith Building at Second and James. For years, he paid more property taxes than any other resident of King County.

Dr. Gideon A. Weed, a graduate of Rush Medical College, came to Seattle in 1870 and developed a large practice. In 1874, he established a private hospital that charged only moderate prices and therefore was awarded the county contract to care for indigents. He was twice elected mayor of Seattle (1876 and 1877). He was also elected the first president of the King County Medical Association. For a time, his partners were his nephew, Dr. Park Weed Willis, and Dr. Franz H. Coe.

Dr. Thomas T. Minor was born in the East Indies, graduated from Yale Medical School in 1867, and the following year settled in Port Townsend, where he served several terms as mayor. He took over the Marine Hospital in that city. He also invested in Seattle real estate, from which he profited greatly in the 1880s. He moved to the growing city in 1882 and five years later was elected mayor. He helped write the Washington State constitution in 1889. A few months later he drowned in Puget Sound while on a hunting trip.

Dr. Alfred B. Kibbe graduated from the University of Buffalo in 1880 and eight years later appeared in Seattle. He was an eye, ear, nose and throat specialist, but his exceptional memory allowed him to discuss other specialties as well. When bacteriology gained prominence in the 1890s, Kibbe went to Austria for a year to study the new science and when he returned was employed as the state's first bacteriologist. He introduced many of the state's physicians to micro-organisms. He also set up the first crude x-ray in Seattle. In 1895, he was named chairman of the first medical-surgical board of Seattle General Hospital.

Dr. James B. Eagleson served at the Marine Hospital in Port Townsend beginning in 1885. He was then transferred to Seattle, where he also practiced privately on the side. He was a charter member of the King County Medical Society and in 1889 was an incorporator of the new state medical society. He was a founder of the College of Surgeons and was the first Seattle M.D. to devote his practice to surgery. He served as medical director of the Northern Life Insurance Company from its origin until his death. As

World War I nurses stand for inspection in Seattle in 1918.

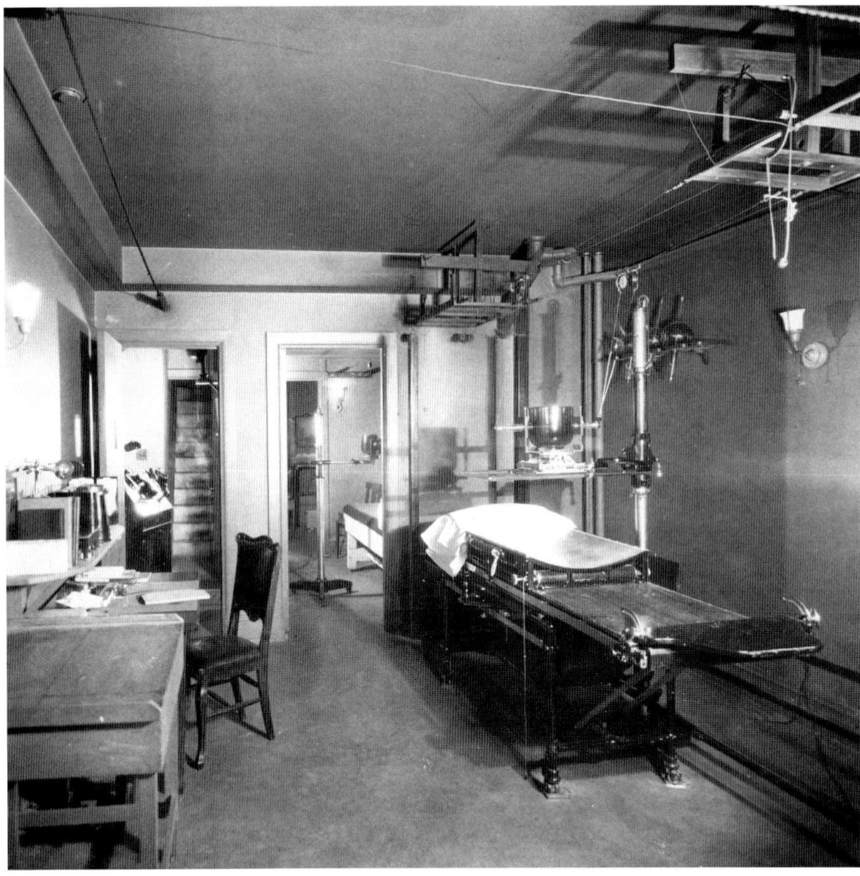

The x-ray room at Virginia Mason Hospital in 1923.

Virginia Mason Hospital as it appeared in 1926.

a member of the Medical Reserve Corps during World War I, Eagleson organized and administered Base Hospital No. 50, which saw active duty in France.

Providence Hospital, one of Seattle's first hospitals, was founded by the Sisters of Providence. The first three sisters arrived in Seattle in 1877 to take over the Poor Farm in Georgetown. The following year, they moved to the Moss home at Fifth and Madison. Mother Joseph convinced Mr. and Mrs. Orange Jacobs to sell them a nearby block on which to construct a hospital. It opened in 1882.

The hospital served as a barometer of Seattle's growth and was constantly being enlarged and modernized. In September 1911, the new Providence opened at 17th and Jefferson, where it is located today, although much enlarged.

Many of Seattle's other hospitals also have interesting histories. Children's Orthopedic Hospital and Medical Center is one of the most notable. It would not exist were it not for a group of wealthy community leaders.

Shortly after the James Clise family came to Seattle from Denver in 1889, their five-year-old son died of inflammatory rheumatism. The mother, Anna Clise, true to her Mennonite training, decided to ease the suffering of sick and crippled children in his memory. She began researching how other cities cared for sick children. In 1907, she called 23 women friends to a meeting at the Chamber of Commerce. All agreed to help found a hospital for children.

They originally opened a seven-bed ward in Seattle General Hospital. The all-woman board agreed to accept any child, regardless of race, religion or the parents' ability to pay. Before

In 1926, Mayor Bertha Landes presented a radio to children in the Theodora Home.

long, there was a waiting list.

James Clise and 20 other husbands each pledged $1,000 toward a new building—a 12-bed facility atop Queen Anne Hill. By now, other women had joined the effort and serious fundraising was undertaken. An epidemic of diptheria was followed by influenza in 1918; both struck young people hardest. Expansion was again needed. When a polio epidemic swept through Seattle in 1924, many children needed long-term hospitalization. Rotary Clubs raised $25,000 for a new wing.

With insufficient space to enlarge further on Queen Anne Hill, the trustees found a new site in Laurelhurst. More than $3.5 million was raised and in 1953 the first patients were moved to the new Children's Orthopedic, which has since been enlarged several times.

*   *   *

In territorial days, lawyers performed double duty—developing local laws and regulations and then assuring their legality under federal regulations for territories. Most civil cases decided by early territorial courts involved interpretation of political questions or legal procedures rather than the rights of parties in the case.

Lawyers were also heavily involved in real estate matters as federal lands were transferred in rapid order to private ownership through various land laws. Many of these early cases concerned questionable land grants to the Northern Pacific Railroad and to logging companies.

Most early lawyers were either young graduates of eastern schools, proteges of eastern lawyers or federal appointees to territorial judicial positions.

The first district court session in Seattle in 1854 found Chief Justice Edward Lander of the territorial supreme court on the bench. Dr. David Maynard acted as clerk (he was also the first justice of the peace in Seattle). No

Anna Clise, founder of Children's Orthopedic Hospital.

Butterworth Mortuary, one of Seattle's pioneer businesses, used this horse-drawn hearse at the turn of the century. The company's roots go back to 1886.

jury cases were brought to trial. The major event of the session was the admission to citizenship of the Dutch settler Henry Van Asselt.

George N. McConaha, the first lawyer to settle in Seattle, was a skilled orator and good citizen. According to prohibitionist Arthur Denny, McConaha fought a drinking problem. McConaha served as chairman of the first session of the territorial council (senate) and after the closing session was physically transported to a party on the shoulders of celebrating fellow members. On the way home from Olympia the next day, his canoe capsized in a storm and Seattle's first lawyer was drowned.

Lawyers played a role in obtaining a rail terminus for Seattle, in securing statehood and in nearly every other local history-making activity. As the population in general increased, so did the complexity of the law and the number of lawyers.

John J. McGilvra practiced law in Chicago then came to Olympia in 1861 after President

Abraham Lincoln appointed him U.S. attorney for Washington Territory. He purchased several hundred acres on the shores of Lake Washington, which are halved today by the eastern end of Madison Street. He surveyed this street and opened it in 1865. He then subsidized the Madison

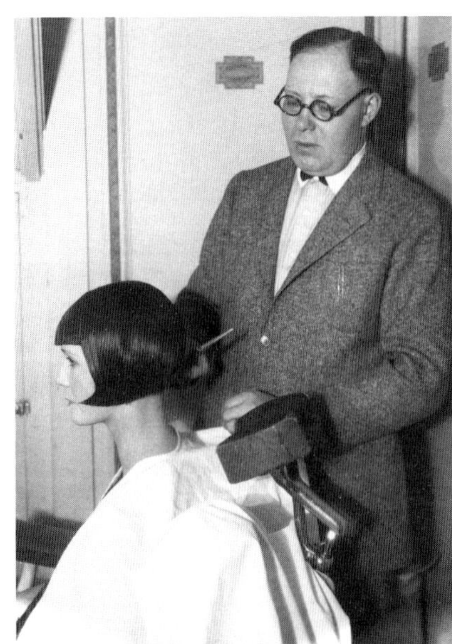

Among the world's oldest service businesses are barbershops and beauty parlors. Back in 1928, Suger's hair bobs were all the rage.

Street cable car line that ran to his property. He later served in the territorial legislature and as Seattle city attorney.

Elwood Evans was an author and historian as well as a lawyer. he settled in Olympia in 1851 and later lived in Tacoma and Seattle. In 1868 he was named territorial secretary and served later as prosecuting attorney, U.S. counsel, member of both state houses, commissioner to the 1876 Philadelphia Centennial Exposition and to the 1893 Chicago Columbian Exposition. He was author of *History of Washington,* published in 1889, and a member of the King County bar.

Elisha P. Ferry of Michigan and Illinois was appointed surveyor-general of Washington Territory in 1869 and territorial governor in 1872 and again in 1876. He then moved to Seattle to practice law and to lead the Republican party. He was elected the first governor of the state in 1889.

Roger A. Greene was appointed by President Grant as associate justice of the territorial supreme court. He arrived in Olympia in the early 1870s and was commissioned chief justice in 1879 and moved to Seattle. In 1887, when his judicial services ended, he became a partner with C.H. Hanford and John H. McGraw, two of Seattle's best known barristers.

During the 1880s, two William H. Whites practiced law in Seattle. The first arrived in 1872 and in 1878 was elected city attorney. In 1884 he was a founding member of the Seattle Bar Association, and in 1886, as U.S. district attorney, he enforced the law during the anti-Chinese riots. For a short time he was a justice of the Washington State Supreme Court.

When the second William H.

Bonney-Watson traces its lineage to 1868, when Oliver Shorey and A.P. DeLin began making caskets at their Seattle cabinet shop. Soon after, they added mortician services.

White arrived in Seattle, there was a need to differentiate, so the first William H., a hulking giant of a man with a booming voice, was called "Warhorse Bill." The newcomer was called "Little Billy." Warhorse married Emma McRedmond, daughter of the founder of Redmond, and took a land claim on the Sammammish River. His home is now preserved in Redmond.

Many of Seattle's law firms can trace their lineage through various partnerships back through the decades to the early part of the century. Short Cressman & Burgess, as an example, was founded 70 years ago by two Seattle lawyers, George Rummens and Tracy Griffin.

*   *   *

Over time, insurance services became more widely available in the region. Originally, all policies were written by companies with offices far from Seattle. After the great Seattle fire of 1889, not only did insurance become more popular, local insurance firms were founded. Farmers Mutual, organized in 1898, was one of these. Its first-year receipts totaled $121. Disbursements came to $76. By the end of the 10th year, insurance in force at Farmers totaled $1.5 million and by the 25th year more than $20 million.

Safeco is a prime example of a modern diversified financial corporation that began as an insurance company. Hawthorne K. Dent founded the company in 1923 in Seattle as the General Insurance Company of America.

Today, we insure much more than did the early residents. No settler insured his family's health or his vehicle. Nor did he insure against liabilities. A little life insurance and a little fire insurance was considered more than enough.

97

Transportation

After Seattle became the terminus for transcontinental rail lines in 1893, Railroad Avenue (now Alaskan Way) became a very busy street.

Most major changes in transportation services have occurred during the lifetimes of our older citizens. They were born into a world when real horsepower pulled the carriages and when long trips were taken by rail or ship. They witnessed the development of autos and airplanes, and watched them evolve into the major carriers of today.

Until the Pacific Northwest became accessible, this far distant corner of America was sparsely settled. The pioneers from the Midwest traveled to Puget Sound overland by covered wagon to the Willamette Valley then north by sail, though a few came by canoe up the rivers and overland to Olympia, then by water to Seattle, Port Townsend and other Puget Sound settlements. Those from the east coast took a ship around South America or sailed to the Panamanian isthmus, crossed overland, then sailed on north to their destinations. No matter how they traveled, the journey consumed six months or more.

The forests of Western Washington were so thick and the hills so steep that land vehicles were in limited use for decades. Sometimes horses were used to carry freight and riders over narrow Indian trails that connected river valleys and crossed over the Cascade passes to the central plateau.

West of the Cascades, the Indian canoe was commonly used. The natives had adapted these craft to the rivers and to the Sound. Canoes came in various sizes and carried passengers, freight and mail.

Thomas Mercer was the first draysman in Seattle. In 1853, he transported two horses and a wagon up a tributary of the Columbia, then overland to Seattle. Where necessary, he and his compatriots widened the Indian trails with their axes.

Sailing ships of various sizes and shapes transported Northwest pilings, lumber, shakes, coal and fish to markets in San Francisco and around the Pacific. Steam-driven paddle-wheelers splashed their way not only around Puget Sound but up the rivers and across the lakes, serving the early settlements.

Many vessels of the mosquito fleet, as it came to be known, were homebuilt. A shipyard would suddenly appear on a sloping beach near a source of lumber. Craftsmen would build their vessels using hand tools. Over the years, some notable shipwrights built some notable ships on Puget Sound.

By 1880, hamlets of every size and even isolated homesteaders were being served by these little vessels, most of which were harbored in Seattle, with its mid-Sound location. This helped Seattle develop into the major supply and service center for the area.

The next major advancement in transport would influence growth and development more than any other before or since. The early pioneers had arrived at a time when the railroads were beginning to prove their worth in the populated regions of the east. These settlers, upon arrival on Puget Sound, began agitating for railroad service. In fact, the first territorial governor, Isaac I. Stevens, a West Point-trained engineer, was commissioned to survey potential northern rail routes in 1853 as he made his way across the continent to his new job in Olympia. But the population was too small and the mountains too high for the railroad companies to give the Northwest serious consideration. The rails were first pushed across the southern plains toward California. The Union Pacific began serving San Francisco in 1869.

Nearly two decades would pass before the first rail service reached Puget Sound directly. In 1864 the Northern Pacific received

Dugout canoes provided the first transportation for Puget Sound pioneers. The first legislators from Seattle were paddled to Olympia in 1853 by Native Americans.

Thea and Andrew Foss founded Foss Launch and Tug in Tacoma in 1899.

its charter to build from Lake Superior to the Sound. Construction began in 1870 and in 1873 Tacoma was selected as the terminus, much to the displeasure of Seattleites. To avoid building over the mountains, the first tracks were laid along the Columbia River gorge to Portland. A recession then hindered progress for nearly a decade. Not until 1883 was activity resumed. A spur line was extended down the Columbia to a ferry that carried trains across the river to Kalama ("where rail meets sail") and from there the tracks continued north to Tacoma.

Meanwhile, Seattle boosters had built a narrow gauge line of their own to the coal fields at Renton and Newcastle. Later, a third rail was added to allow that little line to become part of the Northern Pacific spur serving Seattle. But the N.P. board was partial to Tacoma, where the railroad owned most of the properties; service to Seattle was irregu-

The Seattle-based ships of the "mosquito fleet" soon developed routes to serve every hamlet on Puget Sound.

Small ferries crossed Lake Washington to serve the eastern suburbs. By 1915, gasoline vehicles were competing at the docks with horse-drawn conveyances.

to extend his transportation system from Seattle to the Orient.

The Alaska Gold Rush that began in 1897 placed extreme pressure not only on the railroads that were delivering hoards of prospectors to Seattle every week, but also on the shipping services between Puget Sound and Alaska. During those years, Seattle gained recognition as the major port serving the far north.

For more than half a century, the rails were the principal carriers of both passengers and freight to and from Puget Sound. By the 1920s, however, competing means of transportation were beginning to make inroads on what had been a land travel monopoly. By then automobiles and trucks were speeding over an expanding highway system and air travel was being established between major cities.

lar at best. Seattleites secured eastern funding to build tracks east and north to the newly completed Canadian Pacific. Those were the days when the term "Seattle Spirit" was born.

In 1887, the Northern Pacific built over the Cascades at Stampede Pass and the following year completed the tunnel that allowed the steep switchback tracks at the summit to be avoided. Once the tracks were completed, the railroad began an advertising campaign that sharply increased the number of immigrants to the Puget Sound country. In 1880, newcomers had numbered only 67,000. In 1889, the year of statehood, more than 239,000 new residents arrived.

In 1893, the first Great Northern train steamed over Stevens Pass and through the new town of Everett to Seattle. James J. Hill, the genius behind the Great Northern, did all this without federal land grants. He also built two ships, the largest in the world,

Dedication day in 1948 drew crowds to the Seattle-Tacoma airport.

Mercer Island Floating Bridge

Lake Washington is about 20 miles long, nearly four miles across, and has a maximum depth of about 220 feet. Until 1920, no one could find a way to build a bridge across it. That year, a young engineer named Homer Hadley, an employee of the Seattle School District, noticed some wooden ship hulls left over from World War I anchored side-by-side. They reminded Hadley of concrete barges he had read about. Suddenly, the thoughts in his mind meshed. Why not build hollow floating concrete barges with a roadway on top and stretch them end to end across the lake? He could find no one to take him seriously.

Some Mercer Islanders, tired of driving around the south end of the lake to the old wooden East Channel Bridge, a distance of more than 23 miles, suggested that some of the surplus wooden hulls be used as pontoons for a bridge from Seward Park to the island. At first, no one of authority was interested.

In 1924, after a "Build the Bridge" campaign was waged, Puget Sound Bridge and Dredging Co. prepared plans for a $1 million toll suspension bridge from Seward Park to Mercer Island. The plan was then placed on hold while the company sent an engineer to study a steel pontoon bridge across the Golden Horn in Turkey.

Others suggested boring a tunnel under the lake, but the cost, estimated at $12 million, seemed prohibitive.

In 1937, the Washington State Toll Bridge Authority was created. By then, Homer Hadley was an engineer with the Portland Cement Association. He called on Lacey V. Murrow, director of state highways. Hadley explained that he thought the best route for a floating bridge would be from the Mount Baker district to Mercer Island. The state agreed, but the citizens of the Mount Baker community did not want the bridge approach intruding into their neighborhood. It was decided to tunnel through the hill.

The state, meanwhile, had applied for federal assistance, and in 1938 the Public Works Administration allocated $1.5 million for a bridge, but mistakenly allotted it for the Seward Park route. This was cor- rected and on December 17, 1938, ground was broken and Puget Sound Bridge and Dredging commenced construction. The first Lake Washington Floating Bridge (officially the Lacey V. Murrow Bridge) was dedicated on July 2, 1940. At the time, it was the largest pontoon structure of its kind in the world.

The total cost of the 6.5-mile project, including approaches, was $8.9 million, of which $5.5 million was raised through a bond issue repaid with tolls.

The Second World War delayed the development of east side communities, but after 1945, Bellevue, Kirkland, Redmond, Issaquah and other towns now just a bridge-length from Seattle began their rapid growth.

This photo looks west across the first Lake Washington floating bridge shortly after it opened. The bridge changed the routes taken by many Seattle drivers.

Communications

The *Columbian*, Washington's first newspaper, was founded in Olympia in 1852 at the behest of a number of leading settlers living north of the Columbia River. The reason became apparent in the second issue on September 18, 1852. A number of copies were sent east for distribution among the western-bound wagon trains.

The lead editorial read:

"Come and let us reason together. The Willamette Valley is already full. All the first, second, third, and fourth rate claims are occupied and being improved.

"Will you who have suffered the toil and privations of a 2,000 miles journey in search of a desirable home consent to take the refuse lands of those who have gone before?"

The territory *north* of the Columbia, the article continued, consisted of "thousands of acres of the choicest lands, unoccupied, and waiting for the subduing hand of the agriculturist." Puget Sound, it said, was the safest harbor in the world with facilities to serve ships from the markets of all nations. It predicted, and rightly, that the world's lumber trade would center on the Sound and that, because of its strategic location, the nation's greatest navy yard would someday be established there. It also advised that this great inland sea would someday attract a great transcontinental railroad.

The *Columbian* was also devoted to dividing off Northern Oregon as a separate territory.

Seattle's first newspaper, a

The Seattle Post-Intelligencer *is one of Seattle's oldest businesses. It traces its lineage to the* Gazette, *a weekly publication that over time combined with several other papers. It was later called the* Intelligencer *and was issued from the building shown in this pre-1881 photo. That year, the* Intelligencer *merged with the* Post *and the names were combined.*

tiny four-page sheet called the *Gazette*, began publishing in 1863. The *Seattle Post-Intelligencer* traces its lineage to this little paper.

In 1886 Leigh S.J. Hunt acquired control of the paper and gave it metropolitan aspects. Its influence aided the selection of former territorial governor Watson D. Squire as one of the new state's first two senators.

Hunt lost control of the paper during the panic of 1893 and in 1899 John L. Wilson acquired the daily with a $350,000 loan provided by railroad magnate James J. Hill. The *P-I* suffered through financial problems until 1921, when it was secured by William

Randolph Hearst. The Hearst Company still publishes it.

The Seattle Times also had a history of underfunding and of changing ownership until 1896, when it was acquired by Colonel Alden J. Blethen. Blethen's strong character not only brought financial stability but lent itself to the paper. Blethen descendants still publish the *Times*.

Several other papers made a name for themselves in Seattle, but have since stopped publishing. In 1899 the *Seattle Star* was founded by E.W. Scripps. Other dailies and weeklies have come and gone—the *Argus* and many neighborhood weeklies are examples.

Today the Seattle metropolitan district supports several regional dailies, including *The Daily Journal of Commerce*, the *Journal American* and the *Everett Herald* plus several weekly publications, among them the *Seattle Weekly*, the *Puget Sound Business Journal* and neighborhood papers.

*   *   *

Telegraph wires reached Seattle on October 26, 1864, and the *Gazette* printed Seattle's first up-to-date Civil War dispatches the next day. The wires were extended north from San Francisco to Seattle long before the population warranted the expense of the construction. The first Western Union Atlantic cable had failed shortly after it was laid. As a result, the company planned to reach Europe by way of Alaska, Siberia and Asia. After the wires were extended nearly 600 miles into British Columbia, the second Atlantic cable was laid successfully, killing the Siberia plan.

With the Seattle population still in the hundreds, the area did not generate enough business to

Today, under a joint operating agreement, both the P-I *and* The Seattle Times *are printed on these big presses at the* Times. *The newspapers remain editorially independent, however.*

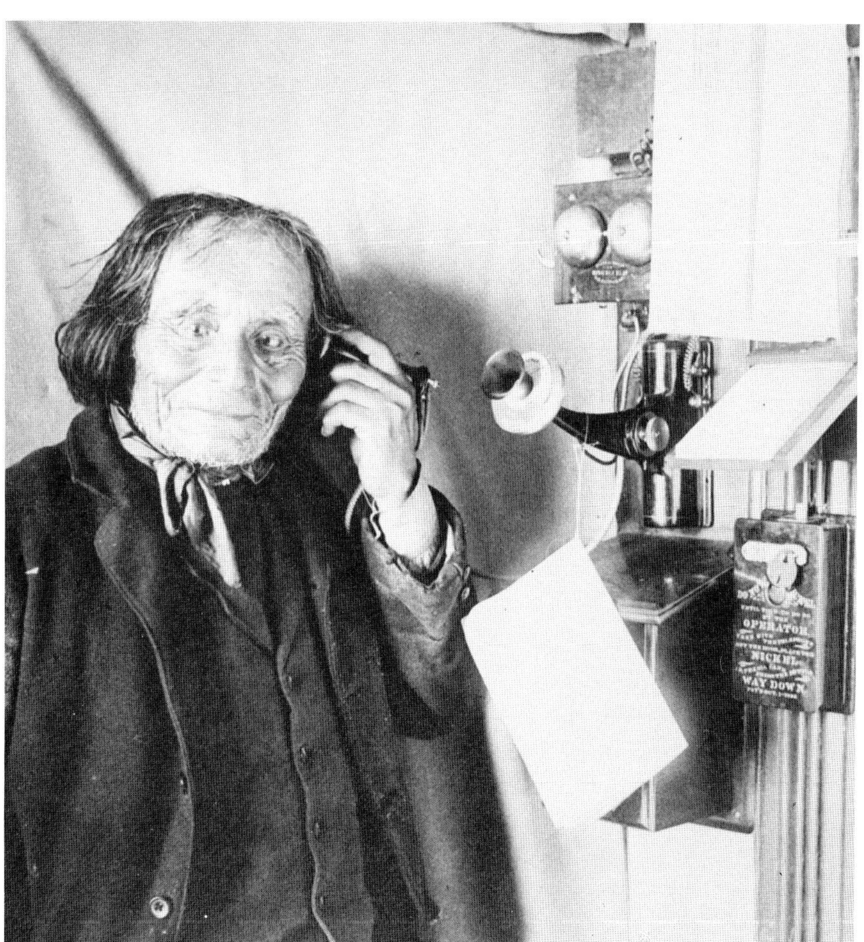

In 1900, noted photographer Anders Wilse captured this image of a Native American using a telephone. This was one of the first models of a pay phone. Notice the nickel slot to the right.

Until the first dial phones were installed in Seattle in 1923, all calls went through "central," which would manually connect the caller to the number requested.

Sunset acquired the Independent company and this inconvenient double service ended.

*   *   *

Vincent I. Kraft is credited with piecing together Seattle's first vacuum tube radio transmitter. The year was 1921. He tested his five watts by playing phonograph records and having a neighbor boy play his violin before the microphone. A few nearby crystal set fans listened in. In 1922, the federal government began to regulate transmission and require broadcasting licenses. Kraft was granted the call letters KJR.

The *Post-Intelligencer* also built a five-watt transmitter in a shack atop its building and late in 1921 began broadcasting nightly news summaries. Other stations were soon competing for air time, among them Father Sebastian Ruth at St. Martin's College near Olympia; J.D. Ross, who built a station in the dome of Seattle's First Presbyterian Church; and

pay the costs of maintaining the line. During the 1873 recession, the company planned to discontinue service north of Portland. Eighteen Puget Sound businessmen, mostly mill owners who relied on the telegraph for lumber orders from California, subscribed to $1,800 in advance tolls in order to keep the line functioning. Thus Seattle hung onto its telegraph service. Within two decades the city was large enough to attract competing services from Postal Telegraph.

The first telephone was demonstrated in Seattle in 1876, using the telegraph wire to Freeport (West Seattle). Not until eight years later, however, was the first telephone exchange opened by E.W. Melse of Sunset Telephone Company, now US WEST. In 1900, a second service, Independent Telephone, came to town. For 12 years, Seattleites had their choice of two companies that were not connected in any way. Most businesses were forced to lease services from both in order to reach their customers. In 1913,

KFQX was financed by rum-runner Roy Olmstead. Its transmitter was located in a bedroom in Olmstead's Ridgeway Place home in Seattle. It began operating in 1924 with the late Nick Foster (seen in the photo) as engineer.

Louis Wasmer, who put together a transmitter atop Rhodes Department Store.

In 1924, Roy and Elise Olmstead paid Al Hubbard to build a 600-watt station in their home. With the call letters KQFX, it attracted many listeners. Elise, as "Aunt Vivian," read bedtime stories for the kiddies. Her husband, a former Seattle police lieutenant, was Puget Sound's most successful bootlegger during Prohibition. He eventually would spend time on McNeil Island.

In 1925, the Olmsteads leased KQFX to Birt Fisher. Later it was taken over by Vincent Kraft, who changed the call letters to KXA. But Birt Fisher had radio in his blood and felt an urgent need to become operator of a new station. He decided to call on O.D. Fisher (no relation) of the Fisher flour milling company. O.D., it so happened, was also fascinated with the new medium. Soon, with O.D.'s financial backing, KOMO was broadcasting. Within a few months, in those days of live broadcasting, the station was the

Because recordings were not yet electronic, their quality was poor. Therefore, live musicians were preferred. This dapper pianist (name unknown) performed on KFOA in 1924.

largest employer of musicians in the state.

Late in the 1920s, networks began feeding programs all across the country. Radio was here to stay.

World War II delayed the advent of television in America. Palmer Lieberman's KRSC-TV was Seattle's first television station. Its first broadcast was of the state high school football championships on Thanksgiving Day, 1948. About 1,000 TV sets in the area tuned in. But the backers of the station were short on funds and decided to sell. Dorothy Bullitt purchased it and changed the call letters to match her radio station KING.

The Federal Communications Commission froze television licenses for a time, but once the freeze was lifted, KOMO-TV began broadcasting, as did television stations KTNT, KMO and KVOS. They were followed by Educational Channel KUOW and KIRO-TV.

Today, viewers see instantaneous worldwide news coverage, thanks to technologies undreamed of a decade or two ago—developments such as satellite transmission, cellular telephones and fax machines.

Radio, when it was new, was used in many ways. Here in 1925 is the radio car of the Great Northern Railroad. Passengers could listen on earphones as they crossed the country.

Utilities

Seattleites have been using gas for well over a century. In 1874, John Collins, who owned the Occidental Hotel and that year served as Seattle's mayor, decided that the town's 2,000 inhabitants should have gas lighting. He convinced Arthur Denny, Dexter Horton and Charles Burrows to invest with him. The city council granted them an exclusive 25-year franchise.

A rudimentary plant to capture the gas from burning coal was erected near the site where Union Station stands today. From a small tank, the gas was fed to five street lamps and 42 private users. It was said that lighting with gas rather than coal oil moved a family up a step in the social register.

In the early 1880s, as the population was approaching 10,000, a larger gas supply was needed. Collins convinced Captain Renton, John Leary and others to join with the original group to build a larger plant and extend the lines. At that time, with rumors rampant out of Europe about a revolutionary new source of light, shareholders renamed the company "Seattle Gas and Electric Light Company." The entire town watched as the new facilities were built.

By 1892, several small gas and electric companies were competing. Lawyer Samuel Hill, who would make Seattle his home, organized a company that soon merged with the older utility. In 1901, J.W. and H.R. Clise and C.R. Collins, with funding from William Nottingham and L.C. Smith of Syracuse, New York, entered the competition with Citizens Light and Power Company, which was the first to furnish gas to Capitol Hill.

In 1904, these companies

The repair crew of Seattle Electric Company (now Puget Power) in action in 1900.

were combined as Seattle Lighting and Rufus C. Davis of Chicago acquired the company.

Because the railroads wanted to acquire the tideflat area for depots, the gas company found a new location on the north shore of Lake Union, a site now called "Gasworks Park." Although coal gas was still produced, a new carbureted water-gas generator was installed. Gas technology would advance rapidly with improved generating methods and new appliances such as kitchen ranges, water heaters and refrigeration units.

During the Depression, Seattle Lighting reverted to a holding company and became Seattle Gas. By 1937, the Lake Union plant was producing 6.6 million cubic feet of gas per day from heavy oil and coal. In many parts of the country, natural gas was being used. N. Henry Gellert, president of the gas company in 1950, launched a campaign to pipe natural gas to Puget Sound users.

In 1955, Seattle Gas merged with Washington Gas and Electric of Tacoma to become Washington Natural Gas Company. Late in 1956, after 124,500 appliances had been adjusted to accept the new fuel, natural gas flowed to the area. Increasing numbers of customers have been using this natural fuel ever since.

Gas is used today by Seattle Steam Co. to generate steam for heating many downtown buildings. The company, almost a century old, also uses bunker oil and electricity to generate steam.

Electricity remained an untamed power until the final quarter of the last century. In 1886, electric power first lit Seattle's streets. This Edison three-wire direct current system was installed by Sydney Z. Mitchell and F.H.

Builders of 96 percent of the new single-family homes in the Seattle area install natural gas heating where they have a choice of energy.

A Seattle City Light crew working on a transformer.

Above: *Installing the generators at the Skagit River power plant in 1925.*
Left: *Puget Power's repair crew today.*

Sparling, both trained at the Edison laboratories.

Several independently owned streetcar lines were soon powered by electricity, but the depression of the 1890s caused many to fail financially. Investors promptly employed a new type of consulting team—experts in the electric power business. Their names: Stone and Webster.

Stone and Webster quickly realized that a major reorganization of the tiny companies was necessary. Most surviving electric and streetcar companies were consolidated as Seattle Electric Company. Seattle banker Jacob Furth was persuaded to serve as president.

Stone and Webster expanded rapidly and in 1912 formed Puget Sound Traction, Light and Power Company under which they operated four hydroelectric plants, two steam generating plants, light and power distribution systems and even a gas generating plant and coal mine. By 1948, they had absorbed 58 additional companies in Central and Western Washington.

The company soon realized the value of the west's hydroelectric potential. In 1925, they completed the Lower Baker River plant and in 1933 the Rock Island dam, the first on the Columbia River.

In 1914, the company sold the money-losing streetcar lines to the city for $15 million, a sum later negotiated down to $10 million.

In Seattle, the public electric power system had been competing with Puget Sound Power and Light since 1905. In 1950, the city offered to purchase the private facility's distribution system within the city for $27 million.

Puget Power also sold its holdings in 11 counties, in some cases because of condemnation proceedings that forced the sale.

However, the public began to realize the value of maintaining more than one type of electric utility and to appreciate the excellent service of Puget Power.

Both public and private power systems found that increasing demands for service outpaced their ability to provide it. A partnership approach replaced old animosities. Puget Power, with burgeoning suburbs to serve, grew rapidly. It also signed new agreements with several cities and in 1956 built a large general office building in downtown Bellevue.

The demand for electric power has been doubling every decade. Most hydroelectric sites have been developed. Coal burning generators near Centralia and near Colstrip, Montana are feeding power into the Northwest grid. Puget Power (and public power companies) have long preached conservation.

Today, these companies watch for advancements such as superconductors, more efficient motors and new means of generating electricity, that servant upon which we all depend so heavily.

Part III

Corporate Profiles

Greater Seattle Chamber of Commerce

It was a vastly different age in 1882, when 26 bewhiskered members of the Seattle business community with their high celluloid collars and big fat cigars met one evening in April in the old Butler Building on James Street.

There were some big names in that group, big for that day when Seattle's population numbered roughly 3,500 souls—men like Henry Yesler, Thomas Burke, Bailey Gatzert, H.B. Bagley and John Leary, among others.

That gathering 108 years ago wasn't a social affair. These men had business to talk about. Specifically, they wondered why mail bound for Alaska was being shipped via San Francisco and Portland when Seattle was so much closer.

The federal government in that other, faraway Washington, under the administration of President Chester Arthur, had initiated a vigorous campaign against mismanagement in the contract mail system. But these men in Seattle had learned the lesson that their business successors would have to relearn even today—namely that local entrepreneurial self-help was more effective and efficient than reliance on bureaucratic procedure. If they could acquire that mail contract in competition with the San Francisco steamship company that had it, they could bring a lucrative new business to town.

By the end of that evening, the group of business leaders had created a brand-new Seattle Chamber of Commerce. As it turned out, they also later won the mail contract for Seattle. Joseph R. Lewis was named the first Chamber president, Bailey Gatzert was named vice president and C.P. Stone became secretary.

One has to wonder whether these pioneers could have imagined in 1882 what kind of organization would eventually develop from that meeting in the old Butler Building. Or, for that matter, whether they could have dreamed what their struggling little city on Puget Sound would grow into.

Could Joe Lewis have foreseen a Chamber of Commerce, founded to help win a $12,000 annual mail route to Alaska, engaged in a host of business, civic and governmental issues of which trade and transportation are merely a part? Could he have guessed that Seattle would become, 108 years later, the business, industrial and financial center of the Pacific Northwest? It would be like asking this year's chairman to project what lies ahead for the organization and the city in 2089, another 100 years downstream.

Nevertheless, one thing is certain. "Bringing new business to town"—that's what started it all in 1882 in a young, out-of-the-way city that needed new business in order to survive. And that is precisely what has kept the Chamber and the city going over the last 10 decades.

Throughout its history, the Chamber has been involved in nearly every major community issue, bringing together business and public leaders to cooperate and find solutions.

- The Chamber played an integral part in rebuilding Seattle after the 1889 fire.

- After 10 years of lobbying, the Chamber was rewarded with Seattle's own transcontinental railroad connection in 1892.

- In 1927, five major Chamber objectives were accomplished: the $1 million Civic Auditorium, the $5 million Longview Bridge over the Columbia, the $10 million cruiser contract for the Puget Sound Navy Yard at Bremerton, the Seattle Commercial Airport and an industrial expansion effort.

- The Chamber's Alaska division congratulated itself in 1937 when President Roosevelt authorized the construction of the Alaska section of the International Highway from the continental United States to Fairbanks.

- The Chamber's "Save Boeing—Defend Seattle" campaign

Seattle has long been known as a friendly place. Here a policeman directs a 1917 visitor.

in the late 1940s ensured that our largest business remained here instead of moving to Wichita.

- In 1962, the Chamber was a large part of the World's Fair effort.

- After 20 years of hard work, the Chamber was pleased to see the Washington State Trade and Convention Center completed in 1988.

- The completion of Interstate 90 in 1992 will mark the end of a major effort by the Chamber going back two decades.

The Greater Seattle Chamber of Commerce represents some 3,000 businesses, making it the 11th largest Chamber of Commerce in the United States and the third largest in the West.

The Chamber is made up of seven program councils, each led by a volunteer vice chair and supported by one or more staff members. The councils include: Trade Development, Governmental Affairs, Regional Affairs, Business Action, Community Relations, Communications and Membership.

Each year, the Chamber adopts a Program of Work that identifies key issues for the organization to focus on in the coming year. Most of these issues emerge from the planning efforts of the councils and their committees. Each position or action taken by the Chamber on a major issue begins with a committee recom-

Joseph R. Lewis was the first president of the Seattle Chamber of Commerce. He had been appointed to the territorial supreme courts in Idaho, New Mexico and Washington before he moved to Seattle to practice law. He became involved with several banks and other businesses.

mendation to the board of trustees. The board, comprised of business leaders representing a broad cross-section of the membership, then reaches a consensus that reflects the business community's overall view.

The Chamber works to help ensure growth and prosperity for its members and provide a better community for all who live here. The Chamber's formal mission statement is as follows:

Mission

The Greater Seattle Chamber of Commerce exists to improve and protect the business climate and quality of life in the Greater Seattle region by:

- Being a catalyst for new, positive ideas and by then working to translate the ideas into action.

- Serving as a change agent to facilitate orderly economic growth.

- Preventing events that will negatively impact the business economy and that may affect the community as a whole.

- Providing resources and services that meet the specific needs of its members.

This region's claim to fame is its social, cultural and natural amenities; it is known as one of the nation's most livable areas. It's worth remembering, however, that these amenities come with a price tag, and someone—individuals and employers alike—must eventually pay for them through salaries and taxes. Today's economy paints the picture clearly: when an economy improves, so does everything else.

The Greater Seattle Chamber of Commerce, as a responsible advocate of balanced regional growth, has kept this fundamental notion in mind for the last 108 years. Amidst all the critical issues in which it has been involved over the decades, the Chamber has consistently spoken out for the legitimate interests and needs of the business community in Seattle and throughout the region. It has won some of its fights and lost others, but like the area it serves, it has matured far beyond anything Joe Lewis and the presidents who succeeded him could imagine.

For over a century, in good times and bad, in war and peace, and amidst all the controversies and squabbles that inevitably arise in a growing region, the Greater Seattle Chamber of Commerce has remained a center of business leadership.

Associated Grocers, Inc.

Nineteen thirty-four was the benchmark year of the Great Depression; unemployment reached its peak and lines at soup kitchens were long. Many an American family went to bed with not quite enough to eat, praying that tomorrow would bring new hope. Times were bleak.

But it was also a time of new beginnings. Nineteen thirty-four was the year 11 independent grocers joined forces to pioneer a new concept in the grocery industry—Associated Grocers.

Under the dynamic leadership of J.B. Rhodes, they established their own independent wholesale company so they could survive the Depression and compete with the chain stores.

From the beginning, Associated Grocers made a firm commitment to keep the independent grocer/customer competitive in every phase of retail operations. As con-

A.G. founder J.B. Rhodes, left, with his son and successor, Willard Rhodes.

sumer demands have changed, A.G. has always been in the vanguard of developing new programs and services for the retail customer.

Even during World War II, when many products were scarce, Associated Grocers managed to provide its customers with competitively priced merchandise and a wide range of imaginative retail services and programs.

In the 1940s, the company was one of the first wholesalers in the nation to offer a complete retail pricing service to keep customers abreast of competitive pricing in their market.

Success had its price, however. The company's warehouse couldn't handle all the business. So, for the second time in just 10 years, A.G. moved—this time into its present 50-acre warehouse complex at the south end of Seattle's Boeing Field.

During the next three decades, the company continued to introduce innovative new services and programs to stay competitive: boxed beef, electronic ordering systems, checkstand scanners,

A predecessor of today's Thriftway and Market Place stores, the Shurfine name allowed independent grocers to cooperatively advertise under a single identity, maximizing promotional dollars.

store decor, site development, market research and a new line of high-quality private label products—Western Family.

Associated Grocers has grown to be one of the largest retail support and distribution centers in the nation, delivering nearly 4.5 million pounds of fresh and non-perishable foods each day to retail customers in Washington, Oregon, Alaska, Hawaii and even the Republic of Guam. It supports its customers with a host of services too, from shelf space management and store format development to product merchandising and financial services.

Through a unique partnership between the retailer and wholesaler, A.G. has helped the Northwest become one of the strongest independent retail markets in the nation. Its customers command an impressive 35 percent share of the marketplace.

Keeping retail customers competitive on a playing field that is not always level is the key to

A.G.'s modern fleet of trucks travels more than five million miles a year.

A.G.'s growth and continuing success.

To meet this challenge, A.G. maintains the commitment J.B. Rhodes made to the company's customers more than 55 years ago:

"We will provide whatever products or services necessary to keep our customers competitive in every phase of the food business at the most competitive prices possible."

Today's supermarkets bear little resemblance to those of five decades ago. One thing has remained constant, though: A.G.'s solid commitment to the steady growth and success of its retail customers.

Milestones

1934

Eleven Seattle-area independent grocers foin forces with founder J.B. Rhodes to form Associated Grocers. Sales top $1 million.

1942

Growth has been so rapid that the company moves to a new warehouse on the corner of Holgate & Occidental. More than 260 retailers are A.G. customers.

1955

The first Miss Thriftway enters competition. Eventually the three Thriftway boats capture three national championships and four Gold Cups during their colorful career.

1967

A.G. pioneers the distribution of boxed beef to retailers. The vacuum sealing process enhances product flavor and freshness.

1975

The Northwest's first electronic scanners are installed in an A.G. customer's store, revolutionizing supermarket operations.

1989

Associated Grocers services nearly 400 retail customers in Washington, Oregon, Alaska and Hawaii. Sales approach $1 billion.

John Fluke Manufacturing Company

In 1952, a railroad car—Erie box car #82197—arrived in Seattle from Connecticut bearing all the worldly assets of a company that would pioneer the electronics industry in the Northwest. With its arrival, John Fluke, Sr. realized his dream of relocating his four-year-old company to the part of the country he called home.

Today, the John Fluke Manufacturing Company is third behind Hewlett Packard and Tektronix in the manufacture and marketing of electronic test and measurement equipment used in the design, manufacture, calibration and field service of electrical and electronic assemblies and products.

John Fluke, Sr. started his company in 1948 in the basement of his home in Springdale, Connecticut. The following year, he shipped his first product, an electronic power meter, to his former employer, the General Electric Company.

Fluke found success by paying attention to customer needs. He asked his customers how he could better serve them and he listened closely to their responses. "He's the boss," said Fluke, Sr. of his customers. "He's got the right to get a little bit more than he expected."

Recognizing the need for a portable voltage meter that could meet the exacting standards of industrial and aerospace applications, the company introduced its differential voltmeter in 1955. The product used existing technology in an innovative way to meet a pressing customer need. It established a new category of test in-

John Fluke, Sr., the entrepreneur, in the company's first manufacturing facility—the basement of Fluke's home in Springdale, Connecticut.

struments, and led to profitable growth for the Fluke company.

From 1955 to 1963, several acquisitions expanded and solidified the company's position. The acquisition of Rinco Inc. in 1958 brought critical component technology that further established the firm's leadership in metrology equipment. In 1963, Fluke's purchase of Montronics, Inc. enhanced its product line and engineering expertise in frequency

synthesis, a new technology for the rapidly growing telecommunications industry.

Early on, Fluke recognized that Europe and Asia would come to represent huge markets for its products. In 1966, Fluke International Corporation was formed to sell to and serve these developing foreign markets. Today, in addition to its 26 sales and support locations in the United States, Fluke has sales, support and service offices in Canada, Japan and the People's Republic of China. Since 1988, Fluke products have been sold and supported in Europe, Africa, Australia and New Zealand by N.V. Phillips, under an alliance with Fluke. The rest of the world is covered for Fluke by independent manufacturers' representatives. Aside from some assembly in China of products for the Chinese market, all of Fluke's products are manufactured in its plants in Everett.

In the 1970s, the company experienced tremendous growth. In 1973, it purchased Trendar Inc. and Analog Digital Research Ltd.,

The Fluke company's first home after moving to Seattle in December 1952.

gaining entry to the fast-growing electronic production test market and the large electronic frequency counter market. Three years later, the company established its own direct sales operation in the United States by buying most of the domestic companies that previously sold Fluke products as manufacturers' representatives.

An aerial view of Fluke headquarters. A total of 1,900 employees are housed in this facility and two other complexes in Everett.

Since then, targeted-account selling has allowed Fluke's direct sales staff to become more knowledgeable about each customer's needs and to give expert advice on finding solutions for complex test and measurement needs.

The '70s brought huge technological advancements throughout the electronics industry. Even so, Fluke set the industry on its ear when it introduced its handheld digital multimeter in 1977. Using proprietary microelectronics, this $169 unit outperformed bulky and unreliable instruments that often cost hundreds or even thousands of dollars more. Fluke tech-

John Fluke, Sr. holding the company's first handheld DMM. By the time this photo was taken in 1977, Fluke's worldwide leadership in precision instrumentation was well established.

nology became available to everyone with even a casual application for electronics.

According to John Fluke, Sr., "The only way you can survive in this business is to keep growing. If anybody feels they can get to a point and park there . . . they've got to be full of prunes." So the company grew. Fluke topped $100 million in revenue for fiscal year 1979, 10 times its annual revenue at the beginning of the decade. The company's annual compounded growth rate was 26 percent. The value of Fluke stock rose 1,088 percent over the decade.

From 1959 to 1981, Fluke was headquartered in Mountlake Terrace, just north of Seattle. With the completion of its new world headquarters in 1981, the company moved a few miles north to Fluke Park, a half-million-square-foot facility on a 150-acre campus in Everett. The operations of all corporate divisions are integrated here, including one of the state's few microelectronics manufacturing plants.

The early 1980s saw top management changes as John Fluke, Sr. reduced his involvement in the company's operations. In 1982, long-time senior manager George Winn was named company president. After John Fluke, Sr. passed away on February 11, 1984, John Fluke, Jr. was elected chairman of the board.

In late 1983, the company introduced the Fluke 70 Series Handheld Digital Multimeters. Promoted through a very effective network of distributors, one million units were sold within three years. The 70 Series became the world's most popular handheld

With a penchant for picking winners, Fluke company officials host George Bush during his successful presidential campaign. From left to right: Congressman John Miller, Chairman of the Board John M. Fluke, Jr., President/CEO George Winn and George Bush.

Three generations of the Fluke family at the groundbreaking for the John M. Fluke, Sr. Hall on the University of Washington campus. From left to right: Mrs. David Fluke; U.W. president Dr. William Gerberding; Mrs. John M. Fluke, Sr.; John M. Fluke III; David Fluke; Washington State University President Dr. Sam Smith; Chairman of the Board John M. Fluke, Jr.; and Mrs. John M. Fluke, Jr.

digital multimeter. It was this kind of business success that, by 1984, vaulted the company's sales over $200 million.

In 1985, the U.S. commercial electronics industry entered what was to be a three-year recession. For Fluke, sales of big-ticket instruments and systems to large commercial accounts declined as factories reduced capital spending. This was offset somewhat by an increase in government business and the continuing popularity of Fluke handheld digital multimeters. And while sales in the United States declined slightly, a combination of the right products and a weakened dollar boosted sales in Asia.

Fluke has prospered in the face of stiff Asian competition where other U.S. companies have been less successsful partly because of its reliance on in-house design and manufacturing to control quality in many key components for its equipment. The quality of Fluke's products, while well known in the industry, was given broader recognition in March 1988, when *Forbes* magazine identified Fluke digital multimeters as one of the 100 best products made in America.

Fluke is also a leader in applying advanced methods of design and manufacturing. The search for improved efficiency extends to every aspect of production, driven by the knowledge that improvement in this area enhances product quality and performance, reduces cost and heightens customer value.

Fluke has always been in-

volved in the communities in which it operates. Both the Fluke company and the Fluke family are committed to supporting the highest quality of education. Every year, Fluke donates the equivalent of 10 percent of its profits in the form of equipment to colleges and universities. Lyla Fluke, wife of founder John Fluke, Sr., contributed to the Washington Technology Center building on the University of Washington campus that is named after John Fluke, Sr.

Fluke is poised to take advantage of the opportunities that lie ahead in the 1990s and beyond. Its commitment to product development, quality control, manufacturing efficiency and customer satisfaction have made it one of the key players in the worldwide electronics industry.

Pacific First Federal Savings Bank

From its new headquarters in the dramatic 44-story Pacific First Centre in downtown Seattle, Pacific First operates the largest savings bank in the Northwest and one of the financially strongest in the country.

Currently, Pacific First Federal's assets are valued at $6.7 billion. The company continues to grow by attracting new customers, increasing services to existing customers and acquiring other savings banks. At present, Pacific First operates more than 100 financial service centers in Washington, Oregon, California and other Western states, employing more than 1,500 people.

Pacific First's growth will continue with support from an upcoming partnership with Royal Trust of Toronto, Canada, which will provide substantial opportunities for expansion throughout the West.

The foundation of Pacific First's success has been astute management of the change from a two-product savings and loan to a diversified financial services company offering consumer banking products and services for savings, investments and home loans, private banking service, mortgage banking, income property lending, insurance and brokerage services.

An equally important part of Pacific First's continued success is its historical dedication to customer service. The company calls it "Pacific First Class Service." It's more than just a motto—it's the cornerstone of the company's business plan and the standard it applies to every level of the organization.

Pacific First Federal began in Tacoma in 1907 with just $1,000 in deposits. Known back then as Pacific Building and Loan Association, it was founded by a man named John T. Redman and 11 of his friends. At the time, Tacoma was a booming young lumber town with a population of about 60,000.

At year's end, the bank had $2,784 in deposits and one $850 loan on the books. By 1916, assets had reached $1 million. The name was changed in 1921 to Pacific Savings and Loan Association of Tacoma.

During the Depression, Pacific

The bank became federally chartered in 1935. That year, the name was changed to Pacific First Federal.

The Tacoma office was on this site from 1912 to 1963.

Savings and Loan was one of the strongest banks in the state. In 1935 it became a federally chartered institution, and the name was changed to Pacific First Federal Savings and Loan Association.

In recent decades, the bank—now known as Pacific First Federal Savings Bank—has made a number of key acquisitions on the West Coast, among them Auburn Federal Savings in 1970, Spokane Valley Savings in 1973 and Transamerica Mortgage Corporation (of Walnut Creek, California) in 1985.

In a major move, Pacific First's parent company, Pacific First Financial, purchased Prudential Bancorporation in 1987. A key component of the acquisition was Prudential Bank, which was bought for $34 million cash and whose nine branches became part of Pacific First Federal. This was followed in 1988 by the bank's acquisition of Community First Federal and American Home Savings, which added more than two dozen branches in Oregon and Southern Washington to the Pacific First network.

The annual picnic, Benbow Inn, 1928.

Princess Cruises

In 1962, the year of the Century 21 World's Fair, Seattle entrepreneur Stan McDonald went into the cruise business with a single ship—a small passenger liner called the *Yarmouth*. His timing was perfect—his package tours, which rode the crest of unprecedented tourism in the Pacific Northwest that year, were enormously popular. McDonald soon set his sights on a much more ambitious venture: an international cruise line.

In 1965, McDonald chartered a 6,000-ton ship from Canadian Pacific Railway, the *Princess Patricia,* and named his new company Princess Cruises. The "Princess Pat," a former ferry boat, took the first regular passenger cruises to the Mexican Riviera and opened up a promising new market. Princess was the first cruise line to visit Puerto Vallarta, and the first to make regular stops at Ixtapa, Acapulco and Cabo San Lucas.

Princess Cruises added a second ship, the 12,500-ton *Princess Italia*, in 1967. The 20,000-ton *Princess Carla* followed in 1968 and by 1969 the company was running cruises to Canada, Alaska and through the Panama Canal in addition to Mexico.

The 1970s brought uncertainty to the company—the economic recession and the Arab oil embargo made operations expensive and kept many potential vacationers away. But two factors combined to help Princess weather the storm: the company was sold to the Peninsular & Oriental Steam Navigation Company in 1974; and the popular "Love Boat" television series, which was filmed aboard the *Pacific Princess*, gave Princess Cruises—and the industry as a whole—a huge boost.

Princess' reputation for world-

Princess' Midnight Sun Express ULTRA DOMES are the largest, most luxurious privately-owned full-dome cars on the Alaska Railroad.

class service and marketing savvy was a perfect match for the resources and tradition of P & O, the oldest and largest shipping company in the world. By the end of 1975, Princess owned three of the finest, most modern passenger cruise ships in the world—the *Island Princess*, the *Sun Princess* and the *Pacific Princess*—and had added luxury voyages to the Caribbean, the South Pacific, Asia and the Mediterranean. After more than two decades, Princess has

The flagship of the Princess fleet is the Royal Princess, *pictured against an Alaskan background.*

grown to become one of the largest passenger cruise lines in the world.

Under P & O, the Princess domain has broadened impressively. From its modest Seattle-based beginnings, it has grown to approximately 750 full-time employees in Seattle and Los Angeles, plus another 600 part-time employees in Alaska during the summer months. Crews on its 10 cruise ships account for another 4,000 employees, who sail the waters of the South Pacific, Mexico, the Caribbean, the Panama Canal, Alaska, Asia, Eastern Canada and New England, South America and Europe. Although Princess is headquartered in Los Angeles, a major part of the operation, Princess Tours, is still based in Seattle.

Princess' Seattle operation has expanded during these decades as well. Princess specializes in motor coach trips to the Canadian Rockies and the Pacific Northwest, and its motor coach division operates land tours in Alaska and the Yukon. Princess also owns and manages hotels and restaurants, including the splendid 192-room Harper Lodge Princess at Alaska's Denali National Park and the luxurious Kenai Princess Lodge in the wilderness of the Kenai Peninsula. Princess began operating the Midnight Sun Express luxury rail cars when it acquired Tour Alaska, and it operates luxury Ultra Dome rail cars on the Alaska Railroad and beginning in 1990 on Amtrak trains between Los Angeles and the San Francisco Bay Area. The Princess commitment in Alaska is particularly large, with millions invested in various operations there.

Over the years, Princess has established itself firmly as the premier cruise line based on the West Coast. The ever-expanding company continues to open up new markets and introduce its standards of deluxe, first-class travel to new lands.

Washington Natural Gas

Gas service was introduced to residents in Seattle more than 100 years ago by four of the city's founding fathers—Arthur Denny, who landed at Alki Point in West Seattle with the first settlers in 1851; Dexter Horton, Seattle's first banker; John Collins, one of Seattle's mayors; and Charles E. Burrows, a promoter from Salem, Oregon who arrived with much-needed capital at a critical juncture in the formation of the company.

Seattle's residents had their first glimpse of the benefits of gas service in 1873 when it first became available from Seattle Gas Light. At that time, gas was manufactured for one purpose—to provide lighting for the city's steep, ungraded streets. On its first day of operation, New Year's Eve 1873, the company began providing lighting lamps for 42 private users and on five public streets.

The first plant manufactured

During the 1930s, gas company vehicles displayed the slogan "Modernize with Gas."

gas from coal and piped it through the city in bored-out logs. The gas was stored at the plant in a wooden container.

By 1889 Seattle had become the fourth city in the world to operate an electric streetcar system. Knowing that electric lighting was on the horizon, the founders of Seattle Gas Light Company formed another utility, Seattle Gas and Electric Light Company, to produce steam-generated electricity in addition to gas.

Later that year, the city was devastated as the Great Seattle Fire raced through a major portion of the city's business district, destroying both the gas and electric facilities. To serve the new, modern city that citizens were rebuilding, the gas and electric facilities were rebuilt and expanded.

As the turn of the century approached, the popularity of gas increased, as did the number of uses for the fuel. Newspapers in Seattle and Tacoma advertised gas ranges, proclaiming that they provided a "clean, comfortable kitchen to cook in" with a "labor, time and money saving range to cook on." While gas lights symbolized elegance for the homes of the day, the gas range was rapidly replacing wood and coal stoves.

Other products that were part of the modernization of the 20th-century home included gas water heaters, gas griddles and gas irons.

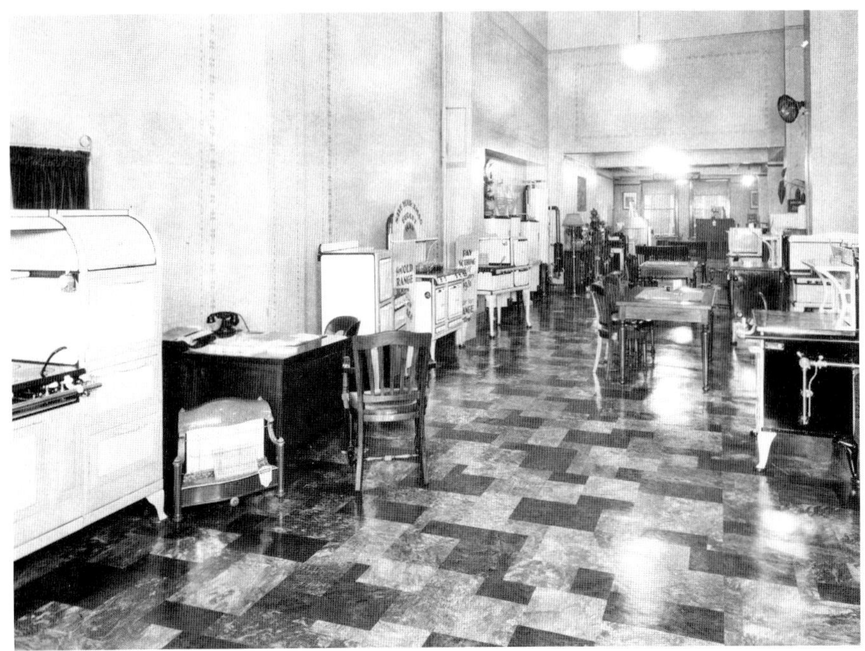

A vintage photograph of a gas company sales floor displaying gas appliances.

During the Depression, the high cost of manufactured gas made it difficult for gas utilities to remain competitive with other sources of energy. In other parts of the country, pipeline transmission companies were introducing natural gas, which was becoming more readily available due to the development of thin-walled, large-diameter steel pipe.

In the early 1950s, a campaign was launched to bring natural gas to the Northwest, and work soon began on a pipeline to transport the new fuel from New Mexico to Washington State.

In 1955, the Seattle Gas Company, serving Seattle, Renton, Kent and Tukwila, merged with Washington Gas and Electric Company of Tacoma, forming Washington Natural Gas Company. By the winter of 1956-57, the firm had made a complete changeover to natural gas.

The arrival of the new fuel was showcased at the 1962 Seattle World's Fair. Natural gas heated, cooled and cooked for many of the structures and restaurants at the fair. A 40-foot natural gas torch burned atop the Space Needle during the fair and for a decade thereafter as a symbol of the gas industry's contributions to the progress of Western Washington.

Natural gas is among the most easily controlled sources of energy, and industries throughout the area quickly adopted it. Industries use natural gas for everything from firing furnaces and kilns to forging, cutting, hardening, drying, purifying, fabricating, processing, curling and shaping materials.

Residents in the company's

In 1936, Seattle Gas Company encouraged consumers to trade their old ranges for new modern gas ranges.

service territory continue to realize the benefits of natural gas today. With a strong economy, the area is experiencing tremendous growth, resulting in record new housing construction. Washington Natural Gas continues to extend its gas lines in response to these growing communities' requests for gas service.

Throughout the area, the use of natural gas in single-family homes is flourishing. Ninety-six

Today, Washington Natural Gas Company's corporate headquarters is located at 815 Mercer Street, a site in downtown Seattle where members of the pioneer Denny family gathered to picnic.

percent of builders of single-family homes insist on installing natural gas heating equipment where they have a choice of energy.

The company is also adding office buildings and retail space to its customer load. Office parks and strip malls are emerging in numerous areas. Many architects, builders, owners and developers are requesting natural gas in these new buildings.

During its fiscal year 1989, Washington Natural Gas has added more than 20,000 new customers, bringing the total to more than 328,000 residential, commercial and industrial customers in five counties—King, Pierce, Lewis, Snohomish and Thurston. The company provides more energy each year than any other utility in the state.

Washington Natural Gas is a subsidiary of Washington Energy Company, which has operations in 13 states, three Canadian provinces and the Gulf of Mexico. The parent company's interests include distribution of natural gas, marketing of energy and conservation services and products, coal holdings, and oil and gas exploration and production.

Federated Group

The man behind Federated Group is its owner and chairman, John F. Gemmill. Born and raised in Seattle, Gemmill entered the insurance business in 1946 after returning from Europe at the conclusion of World War II. After nearly 15 years in the claims end of the business with SAFECO, Allstate and Preferred Insurance Exchange, he started his own general agency in 1960. By 1963, the John F. Gemmill General Agency name had been changed to Insurance Management Inc., which would become synonymous with high-risk automobile insurance in Seattle. It was *the* source for local insurance agents.

Even though Insurance Management Inc. had represented several insurance companies over the years, its greatest success came during the early 1970s while representing Federated American Insurance Company, a small, Seattle-based insurer. Incorporated in 1955 and organized under the sponsorship of the Washington State Federation of Labor, it was financially controlled by the unions, members of the AFL-CIO and its largest shareholder, Wayne Murray.

When Murray decided to sell his Federated American stock in 1976, he offered his shares first to Gemmill, because of their long friendship and business association, which went all the way back to the 1950s. After control changed hands, Gemmill moved Federated American from its downtown Seattle location to his

John F. Gemmill.

building in North Seattle, which overlooks Lake Washington, and in 1984 he bought out all of the company's remaining shareholders.

After gaining control, Gemmill merged Insurance Management Inc. into Federated American. But there was a problem: his general agency was a large writer of high-risk automobile insurance sold through local agents, while his new acquisition was a small writer of low-risk automobile and homeowner policies sold directly, without agents. To resolve this dilemma, Gemmill decided to start Rainier Insurance Company in 1980. This new company was a "direct-writer," and would serve the original Federated American policyholders, plus new customers acquired through referrals and advertising.

By 1984, the Rainier name had changed to National Merit, and the number of policyholders had grown significantly. Federated Group today is comprised of Federated American, with more than 300 independent insurance agents in Arizona, Nevada and Washington, all selling high-risk automobile insurance, and National Merit, which sells low-risk automobile and homeowners policies directly to the public in Washington. Each company has succeeded in spite of the fact that their markets and their sales methods have been totally different.

As early as 1963, Gemmill's three sons began to get involved in his insurance business. Each started by doing the janitorial work, then moved on through the organization by way of the supply room, the mail room, clerical, claims and underwriting departments, and then on to management positions. This training, from the bottom up, has earned them the respect of the other employees and has given them a base of knowledge with which to govern their everyday business decisions.

Terrence, Timothy and Robert Gemmill now manage the daily operations of Federated Group. During the 1980s, they became stockholders, directors and officers, ensuring their continued involvement in the family business. Located in North Seattle since 1969, Federated Group plans to continue its expansion. In the meantime, John F. Gemmill awaits the arrival of his grandchildren into the insurance business that he founded nearly 30 years ago.

Piper, Jaffray & Hopwood

When Piper, Jaffray & Hopwood Incorporated, a long-established Minneapolis-based brokerage firm, acquired Seattle-based Herron Northwest Inc. in 1972, it set in motion a strategic expansion that has created a western regional headquarters with retail sales branches spanning five states.

Piper Jaffray was founded in 1895 as a one-man office in Minneapolis. The art of finance was in its infancy and the retail business as we know it today had not even begun to emerge.

In the years that followed, the growth of the firm was inextricably linked with history. World War I saw Liberty Bonds; the Roaring '20s witnessed frantic stock activity. In the 1930s, hit hard by the Depression, the firm struggled for survival. The 1940s brought World War II and a low level of interest in the stock market. But in the 1950s, the economy and the stock market began a surprising upswing that continued dramatically, with a few exceptions and some corrections, through the next three decades, bringing with it growth, change and intense competition.

Responding to that competition, Piper Jaffray mapped out a strategic growth plan. Forgoing expansion in metropolitan areas already saturated with brokerage firms, Piper Jaffray looked westward, where brokerage services were more limited and investment opportunities were abundant. That strategy led the firm to the Pacific coast and to the acquisition of Herron Northwest Inc. of Seattle.

At the time of the acquisition, Herron Northwest was a seven-

In the 1940s, board markers and runners kept brokers and investors apprised of the latest stock quotations on large chalkboards.

Government Bond Trader Mary Ann Hurley provides an immediate link to the bond market for Piper, Jaffray & Hopwood fixed income institutional sales brokers in Seattle and Spokane.

year-old brokerage firm and the only New York Stock Exchange member with headquarters in the Pacific Northwest. The firm employed 75 people and had annual revenues of approximately $3 million. It also had an excellent reputation for ambition, sales ability and industry expertise.

Expansion in the Northwest began in 1980 when the company opened an office in Spokane. Five more Washington branches opened within five years in Bellevue, Wenatchee, Aberdeen, Lynnwood and Richland/Tri-Cities. This expansion was the impetus for creating a western regional headquarters, which has grown to encom-

pass Washington, Oregon, Colorado, Utah and parts of Idaho.

Piper Jaffray formed Piper Capital Management in 1985 to provide the highest level of investment supervision for institutional and individual investors. It has proven to be an exceptional resource for all of Piper Jaffray's offices. The Piper Jaffray Trust Company, founded in 1989, provides yet another service to investors.

In Seattle, the company has continued to enhance its reputation with full-service capabilities such as corporate finance, public finance origination and trading with over-the-counter and institutional fixed income desks. Of continuing pride is its highly regarded Research Department, whose analysts provide incisive commentary on regional companies.

Today, Piper Jaffray brokers can depend on more services than ever from the Seattle regional headquarters and the corporate headquarters in Minneapolis.

Through the years, Piper, Jaffray & Hopwood has undergone many changes. But each change has been made with strict adherence to the company's corporate mission—to provide the best possible service to its clients.

PSF Industries, Inc.

Founded in 1900, during the Klondike gold rush era, PSF's history is a story of growth and transition in keeping pace with the vigorous expansion and development of the western United States.

Known originally as Puget Sound Sheet Metal Works, the company gradually changed its focus to heavier and more specialized fabricating in steel plate, alloys and exotic metals up to three inches in thickness. As the founding name became less and less descriptive of the versatile scope of the company's operations, it was changed in 1955 to Puget Sound Fabricators, Inc. In 1965, it became PSF Industries, Inc.

The company is presently comprised of two divisions. The Industrial Contracting Division serves a wide range of western industries. Its accomplishments are nearly endless and include the custom fabrication and erection of heat exchangers, evaporators, jacketed vessels, vats, hoppers, pressure, vacuum and storage tanks, and equipment for the chemical, petroleum, smelting, refining, pulp and paper and other industries. PSF regularly undertakes difficult and unusual custom fabrication and erection projects, and has earned a reputation for efficient handling of plant turnaround rehabilitation tasks. In recent years, the Industrial Contracting Division has shifted its emphasis to more on-site erection projects and less shop fabrication work.

PSF's Mechanical Contracting Division, formed in 1976, designs/builds and installs HVAC systems for many diverse regional commercial, retail, institutional, medical and industrial projects, including the mechanical contracting requirements for the majority of Nordstrom's West Coast stores, and is currently involved in Nordstrom's East Coast expansion. Licensed in most western states, PSF Mechanical is geared to give individualized service from concept through completion and warranty.

The past nine decades have allowed PSF Industries, Inc. to become a well-coordinated, fully-equipped organization, built on excellence of performance through teamwork and client satisfaction. The company is determined to remain a flourishing business for generations to come.

A great many of PSF Industries' retubing and emergency repair jobs come from customers of long standing or referrals.

Puget Sound Sheet Metal Works' first plant was located on Western Avenue. In 1906, the company moved to a larger plant on Railroad Avenue, now Alaskan Way.

SAFECO

SAFECO, one of the 20 largest diversified financial corporations in the country, began in Seattle in 1923 as the General Insurance Company of America. Hawthorne K. Dent, the founder, set up the company as a combined stock/mutual company, the first of its kind in the insurance industry.

General America quickly earned a reputation for competitive prices and exemplary service. That in turn led to growth. By the 1950s, the General was serving every state and three Canadian provinces.

In 1953, General America created SAFECO Insurance Company to take advantage of computers and new marketing techniques to compete with direct writers. The new company was a tremendous success. By 1968, the SAFECO name had become so prominent that the corporation changed its name from General America to SAFECO.

During this period, SAFECO began to diversify. It added SAFECO Life Insurance Company in 1957, and in 1967 added mutual funds to the SAFECO family of companies. It also purchased Winmar, a Seattle-based real estate development and management company now known as SAFECO Properties. SAFECO Properties owns SAFECARE, a hospital development and management company. SAFECO started a commercial credit company in 1969, and started SAFECOM, a computer services company for insurance agents, in 1970 (SAFECO has since sold all but 20 percent of that company, now known as AGENA, to outside investors). Income from SAFECO's subsidi-

General Insurance Company Building at 45th & Brooklyn in the late 1940s.

aries now accounts for almost half of the corporation's operating revenue.

SAFECO's total assets now exceed $7 billion, and the company employs more than 8,000 people in the United States and Canada. It serves customers in six regions from its regional headquarters in Redmond, Washington; Fountain Valley, California; Atlanta; Denver; St. Louis; and Mississauga, Ontario, Canada. The home office is in Seattle's SAFECO Plaza.

With sound business practices, state-of-the-art technology and well-timed diversification, SAFECO has stayed ahead of the pack in both profitability and long-term stability.

SAFECO Plaza at 45th & Brooklyn today.

Seattle Post-Intelligencer

Wrapped around the familiar globe atop the *Seattle Post-Intelligencer* building is the motto, "It's in the *P-I*." It's a phrase that sums up the reputation of Seattle's oldest newspaper for thorough coverage of local and world events and hard-hitting reportage.

The *P-I* began in 1863 as a four-page publication called *The Seattle Gazette*. The publisher, James R. Watson, was not known for his journalistic instincts—he ran rambling columns and love poems on the front page while news of the Civil War and local calamities lay buried inside. Unable to make ends meet, Watson sold the paper in 1866.

In the next decade, the *Gazette* changed hands another half a dozen times, and finally hit its stride in 1867, when it was bought by Samuel I. Maxwell for $300. Maxwell changed the name to the *Weekly Intelligencer*. The paper began daily publication in 1876 and in 1881 bought out an unsuccesful competitor, the *Post*. The names were combined into the *Seattle Post-Intelligencer*. In 1886 the paper was sold again, and soon became a major force in the region, which was enjoying a great commercial boom brought by the Klondike gold rush. The *P-I* became the "Voice of the Northwest," known for its tough reporting and community-minded approach to journalism.

In 1921, the *P-I* was bought by the Hearst Corp., which owns the paper to this day.

The *P-I*'s biggest milestone in recent years was the signing of the Joint Operating Agreement with *The Seattle Times* in May 1983. The agreement allowed the two papers to consolidate certain business and production operations; the news and editorial functions at the *P-I* have remained under Hearst direction. Since the agreement went into effect, the *P-I*'s circulation has risen steadily.

In 1986, the *P-I* moved to a new location overlooking Elliott Bay—only the 11th home for the paper in well over a century.

The *P-I* continues to stay on top of all the region's breaking news stories. It captured the eruption of Mount St. Helens and broke the story of the WPPSS scandal; its coverage of the Alaska oil spill and the battle over old growth forests has won widespread praise.

Today, nearly half a million people turn to the *P-I* every morning, confident that inside they'll find hard-hitting news reports, authoritative commentary and complete coverage of the arts, sports and local trends.

Seattle Steam Company

For more than a century, Seattle Steam has been one of the best-kept secrets in town, providing steam heating to Seattle in a dependable, unobtrusive fashion.

The two companies that eventually came together as Seattle Steam were founded in 1893 and 1897. They merged in 1912, forming a company called Puget Sound Traction, Light and Power Co. In the early 1950s, the company's steam plant was sold to local investors and became Seattle Steam Corp. In the late 1950s, Seattle Steam replaced its old coal-fired boilers with a system of efficient, modern generators.

Steam was a preferred heating source up through the 1960s, when fossil fuels were relatively cheap, but it lost ground during the oil price hikes of the 1970s. Still, Seattle Steam managed to remain profitable throughout that difficult period. In the 1980s, steam has made a comeback as an

Present-day steam generation plant at Western Avenue and University Street.

Auxiliary Post and Yesler steam plant circa 1920.

alternative to hydroelectric power, which fluctuates in price from season to season.

The boilers at Seattle Steam's two generating plants switch between bunker oil and natural gas, and there are separate boilers powered by electricity, so the system can use the cheapest energy source at any given time. That means Seattle Steam can offer its customers stable, competitive rates.

Today, Seattle Steam provides steam energy to its customers in an eight-square-mile area of downtown Seattle. Its 19 miles of underground mains carry about 5 million pounds of steam a day to more than 250 buildings, including Washington Mutual Tower, Frederick & Nelson, hotels, five major hospitals, two universities, apartment buildings and other

major buildings. Seattle Steam's biggest new contracts include the Washington State Convention Center and the Seattle Art Museum, which will move to its new downtown home in 1990.

Seattle Steam is growing and diversifying under the leadership of Jim Young, who was named president in 1987. The company has secured a major share of new business during the city's latest building boom. It has also invested in alternative energy supplies, and is currently investigating the feasibility of a co-generation plant.

Seattle Steam's second century is shaping up to be even more successful than the first. As President Jim Young says, "We may be old, but we're not old-fashioned. Seattle Steam is here to stay."

Seattle-Tacoma Box

Seattle Box around the turn of the century.

The great Seattle fire of 1889 is best remembered for the damage it left behind, but it was also the catalyst for many new beginnings, including the founding of the Nist box-making dynasty, one of the most successful family-owned enterprises in the region.

Jacob Nist, born in Kentucky, moved his family to the Seattle area in 1880 and worked in Seattle's thriving lumber industry until the fateful fire at the end of the decade. Since his place of employment had burned down, he and his eldest son, Michael, decided to open up their own business on the shores of Lake Union. They called their company Queen City Manufacturing Co.

At first, the company probably made sashes, door frames and a variety of other wood products. It may have started producing boxes just to use up scrap wood, but by 1905 boxes were its main product and the company's name had changed to Seattle Box Co. It soon outgrew its quarters and moved to what is now the corner of Spokane Street and Fourth Avenue South.

Seattle Box was accessible only by horse team and railroad trestle back then. Photos from the turn of the century show it as the only building in the area, sur-rounded almost entirely by water.

Over the years, the area was filled with dredgings from the Duwamish River. It is now Seattle's major industrial district. Early Seattle Box products included boxes for dynamite and food products.

Michael Nist, who had taken over the reins from his father in 1905, stepped down as president in 1917. Of his 17 children, his sons Ferdinand and Joseph became the new leaders of the company.

In 1922, Seattle Box bought Tacoma's Calef Box and renamed it Tacoma Box Co. The Tacoma operation was kept separate from Seattle Box, and each thrived in its own marketplace. Both companies manufactured boxes for fruit, eggs, fish and industrial products.

The Nists weathered the Depression quite well because they never believed in getting into debt. Many of their competitors folded. Business quickly picked up during the war years, when there was heavy demand for boxes to transport food, ammunition and other supplies. Both companies diversified after the war, and made a huge investment to convert from steam to electricity.

In 1975, the two operations were merged and became Seattle-Tacoma Box Co. A new plant was built in Kent to accommodate the new, larger company.

The fourth generation of Nists—Emmet, Gene and Ferd—are now in charge of the family business. Seattle-Tacoma Box now serves numerous major clients in the western United States, and sells boxes and related products to customers as far away as Japan, China, South Korea and Mexico.

Michael and Robert Nist, sons of Gene and Ferd, are very active in the family tradition of innovation and flexibility to better serve their market. One of the Nist family's favorite mottos sums up the attitude that has kept their business thriving for a full 100 years: "Be sure you're right, then hustle." Five generations of Nists have lived up to that creed and have no intention of letting up.

The Seattle-Tacoma Box plant in Kent.

Short Cressman & Burgess

Short Cressman & Burgess was founded in 1919 by two colorful and legendary Seattle lawyers, George Rummens and Tracy Griffin, both of whom served as president of the Washington State Bar Association.

Rummens never attended college or law school, yet he successfully launched his career at age 21 by obtaining the first conviction of a horse thief in Washington State.

Griffin is still remembered as a "lawyer's lawyer." His talents were held in such high regard that the Soviet Union hired him to defend a Soviet naval officer accused of spying (he was acquitted), and the United States government then retained him as special counsel to prosecute communists in the same court (they were convicted).

Kenneth P. Short and Paul R. Cressman, Sr. joined the firm in 1946 and 1949, after serving as officers in the U.S. Army. They led the firm in its expansion. Both served on the board of trustees of the State Bar Association, and Short served as its president.

From its beginning with two lawyers and one secretary, SC&B has grown to 92 dedicated individuals. Reflecting Seattle's cosmopolitan population, the firm's lawyers come from 15 states and Hong Kong, 30 universities and 24 law schools.

The firm was originally located in the Olympic National Life Building, which was imploded to make way for the construction of First Interstate Center, where the firm is now located. Paul Cressman's office is in almost exactly the same location in

Short Cressman & Burgess lawyers—serving the Northwest.

First Interstate Center as it was in the Olympic National Life Building, but 20 stories higher, reflecting the growth of the firm and the city it serves.

SC&B has grown from a single office with leather-bound books on the shelves and a spittoon in the corner to a major downtown law firm with computers—but no spittoons.

Serving its clients in the expanding economy of the Pacific Northwest, the firm's practice has expanded to include matters ranging

- from demands for payment of a promissory note to multi-billion-dollar litigation involving hazardous waste,

- from an easement for a driveway to the development of a major retail and office complex,

- from complaints about odor from a chicken farm to litigation over the capture of killer whales,

- from contracts between neighborhood businesses to international transactions.

Law is serious, but there have been moments of levity (at least in retrospect). Once, a particularly hard-of-hearing attorney, acting as co-counsel, leaned over and, with reference to a prospective juror about to be seated, "whispered" in a loud voice into Doug Hartwich's ear above an open microphone: "I don't trust that SOB on the end." Despite that inauspicious beginning, Hartwich and his co-counsel won the case. Other memorable events included a divorce client denying that she had the missing money, only to have it spill out in open court from the dust bag of her vacuum cleaner when it was subpoenaed into court (we lost that one), and the bank officer in Idaho accused of having embezzled funds (silver dollars) showing up to pay his bail with a wheelbarrow full of, you guessed it, silver dollars.

The firm is looking forward with anticipation and some amusement to the next 100 years.

Spider Staging Corporation

For over 40 years, Spider Staging Corporation of Seattle has been a leader in the marketing, design and manufacture of high-quality powered scaffolding equipment. Spider's family of hoist-related products are in use every day at thousands of job sites throughout the world, and the name "Spider" is synonymous with the perception of equipment that guides or carries workers along the sides of tall buildings.

Led by a perceptive board of directors comprised mainly of Seattle business leaders, the company has achieved a significant measure of market dominance in recent years. The diverse and talented management team is directed by Wilbur R. Greenwood, chairman and CEO; Jeffry A. Levy, president and COO; Richard A. Carlson, chief financial officer; O. Matthew Jeffrey, executive vice president; and Jerald E. Ogburn, vice president for operations. Greenwood, Carlson and Levy formed the core of The Windswept Corporation, which acquired Spider in the spring of 1986.

One of Spider's major strengths is its unique network of 16 branch offices nationwide for the sale, service and rental of its products and accessories. Most of the company's competitors have chosen to sell through independent distributors, thus losing lucrative rental revenues. The company-owned branch system has allowed Spider to capture a steady flow of rental income, to provide prompt service and to grow and innovate by staying close to its customers.

Today, most major buildings are designed with only modest concern for future access to the outside of the structure. Spider's experienced engineering and manufacturing force specializes in solving the problems of exterior maintenance on new and renovated buildings all over the world. Spider's permanently installed systems can be seen on tall buildings in cities throughout the United States and in locations from Hong Kong to Saudi Arabia to the Soviet Union.

By the fall of 1989, Spider's employee base had grown to 230 people, and serious negotiations were under way aimed at a merger with Access Satellite PLC of London, a pioneer in the field of "ground-up" powered work platforms. The newly formed company, Spider International PLC, would continue to be led by the Spider management team of Seattle. But with a Yorkshire manufacturing facility and a U.K. and European operation directed by the Access group of London, Spider would have the opportunity to become the clear world leader in powered scaffolding systems and aerial work platforms.

Univar Corporation

Univar Corporation is one of this region's great success stories. The company was formed in 1966 with the merger of two Seattle-based enterprises—Van Waters & Rogers, an industrial chemical wholesaler, and United Pacific Corporation, a holding company. The new company was called VWR United until 1974, when it became Univar Corporation (UVX, NYSE).

Now North America's largest chemical distributor, the company operates in the United States through its subsidiary Van Waters & Rogers, Inc. and in Canada through Van Waters & Rogers Ltd. From 1966-89, Univar purchased numerous businesses, most of them in the chemical and scientific supply field.

In the early 1980s, the company began to focus entirely on distribution activities, and in 1984 spun off its malting and corn wet milling businesses to its shareholders as Penwest, Ltd. Two years later, Univar did the same with its scientific, textile and electronic supply businesses, packaging them as VWR Corporation.

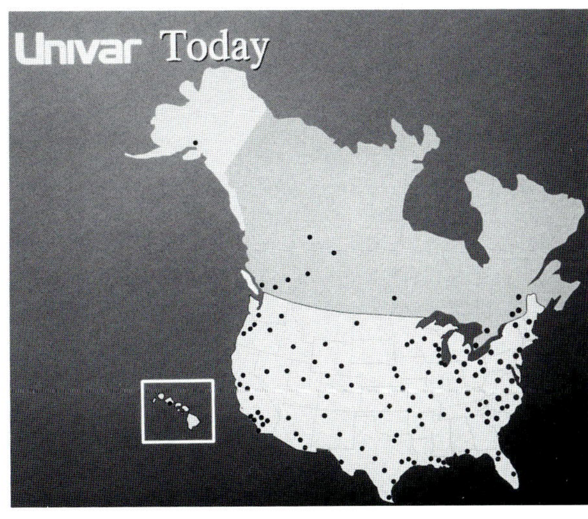

The 1989 annual report focused on Univar's commitment to safe and responsible handling and use of the industrial chemicals the corporation sells.

Serving commercial and industrial markets from over 100 locations in the U.S. and Canada, Univar is North America's largest chemical distributor.

The remaining activities consist solely of chemical distribution operations, which last year produced total revenues of $1.3 billion.

Univar's biggest milestone in this decade was the purchase of McKesson Chemical Co. in late 1986. To accomplish this transaction, Univar formed an alliance with Pakhoed Investeringen B.V., a Dutch company. Pakhoed now owns 35 percent of Univar's stock.

As it looks to the 1990s, Univar expects to continue concentrating on chemical distribution. With a market share of a little over 10 percent of the $12-billion U.S. market for independent chemical distribution, the company is well positioned to provide the increasingly sophisticated sales and service support required by the regulatory, safety and environmental demands that surround its product line.

US WEST Communications

The telephone made its debut in Seattle just two years after Alexander Graham Bell uttered those now-famous words, "Mr. Watson, come here. I want you." The year was 1878 and leading citizens gathered around Colonel C.H. Larabee as he sang "Swanee River" over the wires. The demonstration call, transmitted over Western Union wires, was a great success. Every word was heard eight miles away, in what is now West Seattle, by another group of community leaders.

It was not until the arrival of E.W. Melse in the fall of 1882, however, that the telephone industry really took off in the Seattle area. Melse, a young, adventurous manager from Pacific Bell in California, was charged with the task of establishing the first telephone exchange in Washington Territory.

The company prospered during its first five years. Then disaster struck—the Seattle fire of 1889 destroyed the exchange building and many of the poles and lines in the city's business

Telephone lines expanding across the Northwest.

A 1928 phone installation.

district. All telephone facilities south of Union Street and west of Third Avenue to the waterfront were a total loss. Telephone service was in high demand; the company began rebuilding before the ashes were cool.

In spite of a growth slump during both world wars, telephone companies in the Pacific Northwest continued to grow and prosper. Wartime technology found peaceful uses and in 1952 the Seattle-Portland microwave radio long-distance link was opened.

In 1961, Pacific Northwest Bell (PNB) was split off from Pacific Telephone and Telegraph and became the 22nd Bell System operating company. PNB immediately faced the challenge of providing telephone service for the 1962 World's Fair staff and its more than 9.5 million visitors.

The 1970s saw Seattle's economy go from boom to bust to boom again. In 1977, a record 215,000 phones were installed, and the company invested $1 million per day to meet customer demands.

While Mount St. Helens shook the state in the early 1980s, the most earthshaking event for PNB employees and customers was the breakup of the Bell System. On the first business day of 1984, PNB became a subsidiary of the newly formed US WEST, with 16,694 employees in Washington and Oregon and more than 695,000 access lines in King County.

Change came again on July 1, 1988, when PNB changed its name to US WEST Communications and combined operations with Mountain Bell and Northwestern Bell. The change reflected the company's regional approach to providing telecommunications services in the 14-state territory served by US WEST.

The 1980s have brought great advances in telecommunications technology. The completion of Project Avalanche made Washington the first state in the nation to have border-to-border digital switching capability. The Integrated Services Digital Network (ISDN) makes it possible for Seattle businesses to transmit both data and voice communication simultaneously over the same phone lines.

Whether they have subscribed to Sunset Telephone Company, Pacific Telephone, Pacific Northwest Bell or US WEST Communications, Seattle-area customers have spent the last 100 years calling on their local telephone company for quality service. US WEST Communications has responded by investing billions of dollars to build one of the most advanced telecommunications networks in the world.

E.W. Melse, the man who started it all, would be proud.

Vance Corporation

The Vance Corporation originated as a lumber business in tiny Malone, Washington in 1906. Malone, on the Chehalis River, was a typical mill town, with its company store and company-built housing for mill workers. The man behind the business was Joseph A. Vance, who founded the mill and ran it for 12 years before selling the Malone operation and moving his company, Vance Lumber, to Seattle.

In the big city, Vance began investing in real estate, particularly apartment buildings. In the 1920s, the company built the Joseph Vance Building at Third and Union, the Lloyd Building at Sixth and Stewart, the Vance Hotel at Seventh and Stewart and several other structures.

During the Depression, the company managed to acquire sizeable pieces of vacant land, which it operated as parking lots. The Camlin Hotel at Eighth and Pine was acquired in 1930. During the lean 1930s, Joseph Vance turned the reins over to his son

The Tower Building today.

George, the only one of his five children who had survived into middle age. George remained at the helm until shortly before his death in 1981.

The first existing commercial structure that the company purchased was the Textile Tower at Seventh and Olive, acquired in

1951. The building had been used for textile manufacturing, with most of the products being marketed in local department stores such as Frederick and Nelson. Vance converted it into an office building and renamed it the Tower Building. The Vance Corporation is still headquartered in the Tower Building today.

In the 1960s, the company changed its name to the Vance Corporation, since its association with the lumber business had long since ended. In 1969 it built the Plaza 600 Building at the corner of Sixth and Stewart. During the next two decades, the hotel division expanded its hospitality holdings to include the Hanford House in Richland, The Tyee Motor Inn in Olympia, the Chinook Hotel in Yakima, The Sea Tac Motor Inn in Seattle and the Park Shore Hotel in Honolulu. In addition, Vance Hotels excelled in the field of hotel management with such properties as the Ridpath in Spokane as well as Alaska and Canadian affiliations.

In 1985, a major share of the company was acquired by Sweden's Scandinavian Development Inc. (SDI). A year later, SDI purchased the remaining minority interest and reorganized into two groups: one to own and manage office buildings and the other to own and manage hotels. In 1988 the hotel division, now known as WestCoast Hotels, was purchased by one of the SDI partners.

Today, the Vance Corporation is actively renovating its existing office properties and looks to the future for new development opportunities in the Seattle Central Business District.

The Lloyd Building on the corner of Sixth and Stewart, circa 1930s.

Westmark International

In the sophisticated field of medical electronics systems, Seattle-based Westmark International has established itself as a worldwide leader.

Westmark consists of two pioneering companies that have served the health care community for more than 25 years, Advanced Technology Laboratories (ATL) of Bothell and SpaceLabs, based in Redmond. Through these subsidiaries Westmark develops, manufactures and markets diagnostic ultrasound systems and electronic patient monitoring and clinical information systems.

ATL began as a marine electronics company in 1969 in the Seattle area. In the mid-1970s, with the assistance of the University of Washington, it applied sonar technology to medical imaging to develop diagnostic ultrasound systems. Physicians use ultrasound, or high frequency sound, in such diverse applications as the early detection of disease, the evaluation of blood flow characteristics and the monitoring of pregnancy. It is a painless, noninvasive and cost-effective technology that allows the physician to view in real time a patient's anatomy and physiological function.

ATL's Ultramark® ultrasound systems serve doctors in all major medical segments where ultrasound is used cardiology, radiology, obstetrics/gynecology and peripheral vascular studies. The company has the broadest franchise and the largest installed base outside of Japan of any ultrasound manufacturer.

ATL's Ultramark product line includes many technological firsts for the ultrasound industry. ATL has distinguished itself as the technological leader in the application of digital electronics to ultrasound, an important step toward keeping rapidly evolving technology affordable while offering increasing levels of system performance.

SpaceLabs was formed in 1958 to develop technology for NASA to monitor astronauts in orbit. Ten years later, the company refined this technology to monitor critical care patients.

SpaceLabs has gained a lead-

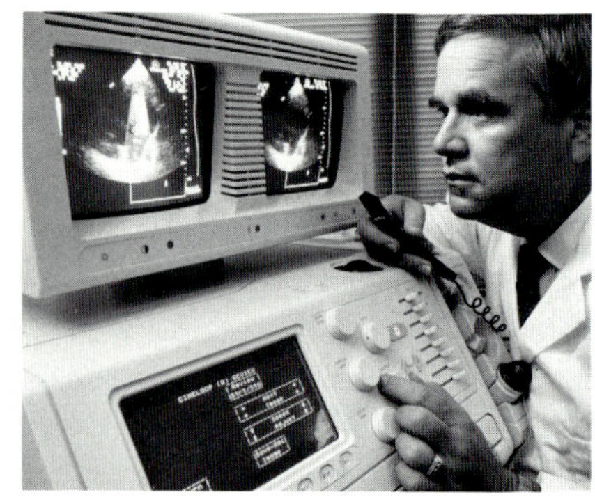

ATL's Ultramark systems incorporate innovative digital technology to produce the most advanced applications of ultrasound, such as color Doppler imaging.

ership position in the U.S. market with its product line, the Patient Care Management System (PCMS). PCMS uniquely integrates critical care patient monitoring with patient information management to form a true clinical information system. PCMS not only monitors a patient's vital signs in the hospital at bedside, it can also be networked to locations throughout the hospital to collect, analyze and correlate patient information. PCMS's powerful capabilities and user-friendly characteristics save precious time and let medical practitioners focus their attention on the patient, not the equipment.

Westmark became a public company in early 1987, as a result of the distribution of its shares by Squibb Corporation to its shareholders. Westmark has extensive research, administrative and manufacturing facilities in the Seattle area, employing approximately 1,800 people in the State of Washington and over 3,000 people worldwide.

Westmark is committed to continuing to provide the medical community with cost-effective electronic systems that lead in providing increasing levels of performance, integration and clinical utility.

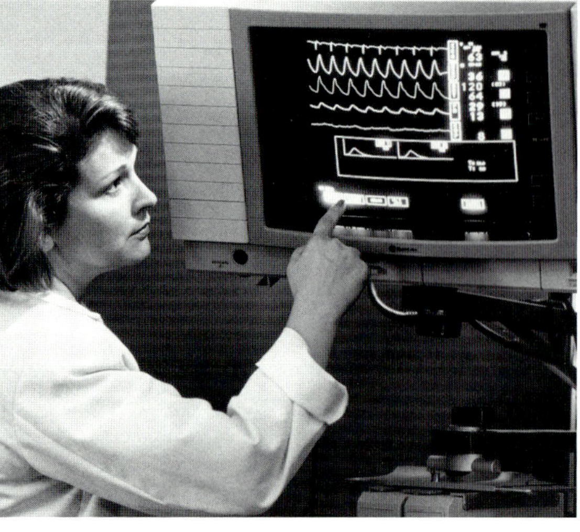

SpaceLabs' revolutionary PC2 monitors critical care patients' vital signs around the clock.